SUPER DOGS

SUPER DOGS

Summersdale Publishers Ltd
46 West Street
Chichester
West Sussex
PO19 1RP
UK

www.summersdale.com

Printed and bound by CPI Group (UK) Ltd, Croydon, CR0 4YY

ISBN: 978-1-84953-622-6

SUPER DOGS

HEART-WARMING ADVENTURES
OF THE WORLD'S GREATEST DOGS

MALCOLM CROFT

summersdale

For Clemmie, and for all the other undiscovered super dogs out there who deserve our love and recognition

CONTENTS

INTRODUCTION

Dogs. Where would we be without them? They are capable of meaning so much to us that sometimes we take them for granted and overlook just how special and unique they really are. They are more than just our pets. Dogs are capable of communicating, caring and consoling us, more so than any other animal on the planet. They are a unique species that can relate directly and expressively with human beings. No matter whether we humans are exploring the highest points on the globe or just relaxing on the sofa on a wet Sunday afternoon, dogs are always by our side. It is with dogs that we share our common (and best) personable traits – our sense of loyalty and love, fun, adventure and companionship.

So, let's take a look at our furry best friends. Let us delve deep into just some of the very best shaggy dog stories about the world's greatest super dogs. From the dogs who have been our lifelines and lifesavers, to the world-record breakers whose brave paws have shown us what real strength and talent is, to the loyal mutts who have shown us what courage and dedication in the face of adversity really requires, and to the dogs who, throughout history, have helped educate us to become better people and learn more about ourselves; and finally, to the dogs who entertain and amuse us, the dogs that make us laugh and smile everyday just by being themselves – this book is a celebration of all these dogs and many more.

Super Dogs is your dogpendium of brave, silly, funny, loyal, heroic and unbelievable dogs who, perhaps against all the odds, have achieved something greater than simply being 'man's best friend'. We are *their* best friends and we need them as much as they need us.

There are lots of super dogs out there, so let's get on with it, shall we?

Malcolm Croft
London
April 2014

HEROIC SUPER DOGS

The history, and hopefully future, of the world
has been full of super dogs, animals that have
gone above and beyond the call of duty.
This chapter is a tribute to them all...

ENDAL

Voted 'Dog of the Millennium' and recipient of the Gold Medal, Endal the male pedigree Labrador became one of the most famous assistance dogs in Britain. You may never have heard of him, so let's take a closer look...

Internationally renowned as the 'most decorated dog in the world' – and not because he likes to wear shiny collars – Endal has been a super dog throughout his long and amazing life and is the shining example of how dogs and people can work together to accomplish simply unbelievable things.

Born in December 1995, Endal suffered painfully from a debilitating joint condition in his front legs known as osteochondrosis, which meant as a puppy his suitability to become a service dog was uncertain. Due to the physical and psychological impact service training has on dogs, as well as the cost and time required to train each dog, only dogs that pass a thorough physical and psychological examination are able to enter into training. With the help of a specialised diet, expert training and controlled exercise, managed by the Canine Partners for Independence, based in West Sussex, Endal was allowed to enter the training programme and qualified with flying colours to become a fully operational assistance dog in 1997.

Allen Parton, a Royal Navy officer, had sustained near-fatal injuries when involved in a car crash during the Gulf War, resulting in 50 per cent memory loss due to severe head trauma (he was also unable to retain memories for more than two days), and was left unable to speak and physically disabled, requiring a wheelchair at all times. Parton's injuries had left him depressed, resulting in a severe strain on his family and marriage. It was during this time that he attempted suicide. The thought of carrying on with life, he remarked later in a memoir about Endal, was just too terrible to contemplate. It wasn't until 1999 that fate stepped in and changed his – and Endal's – life for the better. And all it took was for a bus to be late.

Parton was waiting, outside of his home, for a bus that was due to take him to the local day centre so that his wife, Sandra, could go to work at the local dog training centre (the aforementioned Canine Partners for Independence). However, with no bus in sight, and a job to get to, Sandra took her husband to work with her in their car.

In the book *Endal* (published in 2009), the Partons describe how, when Endal and Allen met that day, Endal took an immediate shine to him, giving him a big slobbery lick and being clearly desperate to sit on his lap! Though Parton could not speak, or show any sign of affection, he too fell instantly in love with Endal. 'It was a cathartic experience which finally gave me the hope I needed,' he said. 'Until I met him, I was in the depths of despair. But when he refused to leave my side at the training centre, I suddenly saw a chink of light.'

Since that day, Parton and Endal were inseparable and the dog went home with him for good, an event that Sandra recalls as the moment their marriage was saved, with them even renewing their vows a year later.

In their twelve-year-long companionship, Endal was trained and taught to respond to over a hundred instructions and many hundreds of signed commands. It was these commands that helped the pair communicate and respond in their otherwise silent world. They also helped Parton regain some independence, as well as live a more normal lifestyle – something that Parton never dreamed would happen again.

In an interview magazine aimed at people with disabilities, for a spotlight feature on Endal's heroics, Parton recounted, 'When I couldn't talk, Endal learned sign language – if I touched my head, I wanted my hat; if I touched my face, it was for the razor. Endal learned hundreds of commands in signing. Eventually one day, in this very silent world we both lived in, I grunted. That was like an electric shock going through him, he was so excited. They said I'd never speak again, but Endal just dragged the speech out of me.'

In their time together, Endal would post letters, empty the washing machine, open doors and operate lifts, pull the plug out of the bath (in case Parton fell asleep whilst bathing), help him get out of bed by pulling his blanket back and swinging his legs round into his wheelchair, pick the phone up and press an emergency button to call an ambulance, gather a knife and fork and plate for his lunch, collect his slippers and the papers from the front door, bark for attention at the bar of his local pub and then pay for his beer, and even – this is my favourite – insert his credit card into ATMs and chip-and-pin machines.

But it was due to an even more unbelievable event that occurred in 2001 that Parton would be forever indebted to the quick-thinking and brave actions of his furry companion. While out shopping in Hampshire, he was knocked out of his wheelchair by a passing car, leaving him lying unconscious on the roadside. Quick-thinking Endal jumped into action and pulled his body into the recovery position (one of the first, and most important, acts a service dog is taught), retrieved his master's mobile phone from beneath the car, fetched a blanket from the wheelchair and pulled it over him, all the while barking to passers-by for help. In the end, Endal ran into a nearby hotel and barked until somebody took notice and followed Endal to where Parton was lying.

This was an event that made a global icon out of Endal – you may remember hearing about it when it was reported in many national and international newspapers, and it is the reason why Endal was hailed as 'Dog of the Millennium' and received the PDSA's Gold Medal for Animal Gallantry and Devotion to Duty – the highest award available to an animal.

Sadly, though inevitably, this story doesn't have a happy ending. In 2009, due to old age and painful arthritis, Parton took Endal to the vet to be put down. 'I knew, of course, as every pet owner does, that this day would one day come,' he said, 'but it didn't make it any easier.'

But Parton, a man who had experienced more tragedy than most, remained positive that he would see his furry friend again. 'When I finally arrive at the pearly gates myself, I know in my heart of hearts that Endal will be there, waiting faithfully for me with his otter-like tail in full swing.'

 There is no faith which has never yet been broken, except that of a truly faithful dog.

KONRAD LORENZ

SERGEANT STUBBY

Sergeant Stubby's story is definitely one of the most uplifting, life-affirming dog tales that you will ever read. He may be Stubby in name, and stubby in stature, but he is a giant in the world of super dogs...

There have been many war dogs praised and celebrated throughout history, from Cairo (used in the operation that ultimately led to the death of Osama bin Laden) to Judy (the only dog to become a prisoner of war), to Just Nuisance (the only dog to have actually enlisted in the Royal Navy), to a veritable litter of other dogs that have, in some barking mad way or another, not only survived the horrors of war, but also helped aid the downfall of evil.

While I am disappointed that I cannot report every heroic super dog that ever lived – that book would be HUGE! – I am happy that there are so many heroic dogs that require celebrating. How many cats do you know of that won a medal of honour during a world war? How many tortoises helped to hunt down, and kill, a known international terrorist? How many budgies... well, you get the picture... 'Sergeant Stubby' is one war hero you may have heard of. 'Stubby' to his friends, was the most highly decorated US Army dog of World War One. This fearsome pit bull terrier mix with a 'stubby' nose is not just the only dog ever to be promoted in the actual US military from 'regular dog' to 'sergeant', but also got to wear a special coat that, after the war, *he had his medals pinned to.* The coat, by the way, was made for him by a thankful Frenchwoman, whose town Stubby had helped liberate from German invaders. The image of a small pit bull terrier wearing a 'uniform' with medals attached to it demonstrates perfectly that dogs can, and should, be treated as equal with humans in the face of adversity; human beings – at a time of great weakness and vulnerability – call on the bravery of the dog to lend a paw.

Stubby's achievements are to this day discussed on TV programmes and news items, whenever a modern dog in some way replicates his heroics. Let's take a look at this stubby super dog's stupendous achievements in action:

- Served with the 26th Yankee Division in the trenches in France for eighteen months.

- Was able to salute his Commanding Officer – a trick the men in his unit had taught him.

- Could understand the difference between Allied soldiers and enemy German soldiers.

- Survived seventeen battles and four 'over the top' offensives into 'no-man's-land'.

- Was injured in the front leg by a hand grenade.

- Survived a gas attack and was then able, by using his powerful nose, to alert his division to new incoming gas attacks.

- Sniffed out scores of injured soldiers lying wounded in no-man's-land.

- Due to his super-powerful ears, alerted his division to incoming shell artillery in the nick of time.

Caught a German spy who was sketching the layout of the US trenches. He was able to pin the enemy down and keep him down until soldiers arrived.

After World War One ended, Sergeant Stubby returned home a hero. A hero that shook the hands of presidents; a hero that led parades; a hero that received many medals of honour; a super dog that had – in his mind anyway – simply done his job.

Don't accept your dog's admiration as conclusive evidence that you are wonderful.

ANN LANDERS

BALTO

When a remote Alaskan village was threatened with an outbreak of diphtheria, there was only one thing anybody could do to help save precious lives – send in the dogs!

Balto, a Siberian husky sled dog, raced to the rescue of a village's children in 1925, when a diphtheria outbreak threatened the lives of every single young resident in Nome, Alaska. Mere days after the last ship of the year had left the residents of the remote Alaskan village with enough supplies to last them during the harsh winter, disaster struck. It was a disaster that would have ended the lives of many – if not all – of the younger occupants. The area's only doctor simply did not have enough medicine to treat this serious, and highly contagious, condition. If enough medicine did not reach Nome in just a few short hours, the children were doomed. The only way they were going to survive was if the relay team that Balto was part of transported the medicine to Nome by dog sled.

The journey was long, treacherous and tiring, with most of the trip spent in total white-out conditions: the type of wintery conditions where it's 'blizzarding' so much it's hard to tell up from down. But the US Board of Health simply could think of no other option.

The teams of dogs and their human 'mushers' raced against the clock. There was no room for failure, no time for delays or mistakes. Balto was the lead dog that had to complete the final two legs of the five and a half days journey, because the final relay team could not be awoken from their slumber in the middle of the night. In total, the teams had covered 674 miles, over a hundred miles a day. Travelling solely by dog!

Thanks primarily to Balto, the children of Nome received the urgent emergency supplies and lived to tell the tale of how a dog saved an entire generation from an epidemic and certain death.

 It's not the size of the dog in the fight; it's the size of the fight in the dog.

MARK TWAIN

BUDDY

The advent of the Internet has transformed the way people all over the globe connect to each other. It has also become a place to share images of dogs in all their glory. But before all this, before the world changed so unexpectedly, an old dog called Buddy was being taught new tricks of his own.

One of the most emotional developments of the twentieth century, I'm sure many dog lovers would agree, was the founding of the 'Seeing Eye School' in New Jersey, co-founded by Morris Frank, the first American to be partnered with what became known as a Seeing Eye Dog – a dog called Buddy.

The Seeing Eye School first opened its doors in 1929 after the visually impaired Frank read an article in his local *Saturday Evening Post* about an American dog trainer in Switzerland, Dorothy Harrison Eustis, who had visited a German school that trained veterans of World War One to work with guide dogs. Inspired by the article in the newspaper, Frank sent Mrs Eustis a telegram, which contained the words: 'I want one of those dogs!'

Frank, in later correspondence with Mrs Eustis, detailed how, in the US, he was not alone. 'There are thousands like me who abhor being dependent on others. Help me and I will help them. Train me and I will bring back my dog and show people here how a blind man can be absolutely on his own. We can then set up an instruction centre in this country to give all those here who want it a chance at a new life.'

Mrs Eustis, touched by Frank's sincere and honest letters, invited him to the training school in Switzerland where he would be paired with a guide dog. Frank replied, 'Mrs Eustis, to get my independence back, I would go to hell!'

Later in the year, when Frank arrived in Switzerland he was partnered immediately with a female German shepherd called Kiss. Mr Frank wasn't too keen on that name, so promptly started calling Kiss 'Buddy'. Frank and Buddy worked, trained and became connected at the heels. Frank fell immediately in love with not only Buddy, but also with the groundbreaking work being taught at the training school.

When Frank and Buddy returned to New York, Frank began alerting the media to show off all the specifically taught skills possessed by his best friend. Up until then, not many people were aware of dogs being educated in this way; guides for the blind was still an incredibly revolutionary concept.

A particularly impressive 'trick' Buddy had learnt was to walk safely across Broadway – one of America's busiest streets – with Frank in tow, a mind-blowing concept to many people at that time. A blind man and his super dog – able to go anywhere they chose, safely and independently; no longer was a blind person totally hindered by his disability.

This fusion between Frank and Buddy heralded the beginning of a new era of professional working relationships between man and dog, one that was to change the lives of millions of people in the USA. Excited at the praise Buddy had received, Frank telegrammed Mrs Eustis back in Switzerland to let her know how Buddy was doing in a busy new city, a city unlike one she had ever been to before. Frank's telegram contained just one word: 'Success'.

From that point on, Frank and Buddy became inseparable, until she passed away peacefully in May 1938. In tribute to the miraculous super dog that had given him back his independence, Frank named all his replacement guide dogs Buddy. He said he owed her so much that he couldn't bear the idea of being without her, at least in name.

And the story doesn't quite end there. Heavily influenced by Buddy's abilities, and indebted to the training school in Switzerland, the Seeing Eye School that Frank and Mrs Eustis created in January 1929 still trains puppies to this day in basic obedience for four months, followed by a month of intense obedience training with their future human partners. With all the circus surrounding the millions of super dogs that show their unique skills and tricks on YouTube and other social media networks, sometimes it's nice to remember that the beginning of what is now the oldest existing guide dog school in the world – a school that helps blind and visually impaired people all over the world regain their independence – all started with a simple telegram that contained the words 'I want one of those dogs!'

 We long for an affection altogether ignorant of our faults. Heaven has accorded this to us in the uncritical canine attachment.

GEORGE ELIOT

LUCKY AND FLO

> Let us now meet a very modern pair of crime-fighting dogs with a truly special talent indeed... it's Lucky and Flo!

As the story goes, around 2004, John Malcolm, the anti-piracy director in the MPAA (Motion Picture Association of America), was trying to come up with new ways to combat piracy. Experts and analysts, those people forever nibbling on the end of their biros, have concluded – with widely varying figures and statistics – that file-sharing and pirate DVDs are costing the music and film industries £3 billion and £1 billion respectively.

Piracy is a real problem. It affects not only the long-term future and prosperity of both industries, but also the larger economies of nations whose companies spend a lot of time, effort, and money creating, producing and distributing blockbusting movies and chart-topping hits. Jobs have already been lost in their thousands due to this serious and complex issue.

So, it's a good thing that Malcolm had a brainwave that – while maybe not *entirely* wiping out the problem – was certainly a dog-step in the right direction. Malcolm's rather savvy, blue-sky, thinking-outside-of-the-box idea was to call upon man's furry best friend in the war on piracy. He must have thought, 'We're screwed... only dogs can save us now!' I don't blame him, it's what I would do!

So, without further ado, please give a warm and smelly welcome to Lucky and Flo – the world's *best*, and *only*, piracy crime-fighting duo, and the world's first dogs purposely trained to decipher the smell of the particular polycarbonate used in DVDs.

Renowned dog trainer Niall Powell specifically chose and trained Lucky and Flo, two black Labrador retrievers, to detect the smell of the polycarbonate. All DVDs, counterfeit and non-counterfeit, are made with this particular polycarbonate, so while Lucky and Flo weren't specifically detecting pirated DVDs with their noses, they were able to sniff out and locate large quantities of DVDs in an area where there should be no detectable smell of that particular polycarbonate. If the dogs got wind of the smell in an area where that smell should not be – say a bottle manufacturer – detectives would know that a shipment or large volume of DVDs was nearby and would have probable cause to search the grounds.

In their unique time as doggy detectives, Lucky and Flo have discovered millions of pirated and counterfeit discs at piracy sweet spots all over the world, and have been responsible for the arrests of scores of naughty people who should know better than to mess with dogs. Never let sniffing dogs lie, that's my motto.

Lucky and Flo are most often deployed out when the MPAA already suspect a warehouse or storefront is hiding an underground, disc-duplication operation or large volumes of counterfeit discs, whereupon the dogs are sent in to sniff them out. In Malaysia alone, Lucky and Flo have assisted in over thirty-five raids, leading to the arrest of twenty-six people and the discovery of about 1.9 million pirated discs, the MPAA has reported.

Lucky and Flo have become so good at sniffing out pirates (as it were) that in Malaysia – a country in dire need of a crackdown on illegal pirating – professional counterfeiters and DVD makers have even placed a cash bounty on their heads.

'Word on the streets,' Malcolm said in a recent newspaper interview, 'was that disc-counterfeiting groups had put out a hit on the disc-sniffing pooches.' Indeed, a yellow Labrador retriever named Manny, another of the MPAA's trained disc-sniffers, died suddenly in 2012, while undercover in Malaysia. Experts suspect the dog might have been murdered because of its involvement with the MPAA. If so, is this the first case of a dog being assassinated? Did Manny die in the line of duty?

The future of piracy, illegal file sharing and counterfeit DVDs is a growing and evolving problem – a problem, sadly, that is too big for Lucky and Flo alone to solve. But by being used as international 'spokesdogs', the two canines have become minor celebrities in the war on piracy. The MPAA have recently taken the dogs on a media tour around the world as part of a public relations campaign to place a spotlight on piracy and there is even a children's book, with Lucky and Flo as the stars, teaching kids about the importance of copyright law and the evils of copyright infringement. I kid you not!

'We undertook this just as an experiment,' Malcolm said of Lucky and Flo's increasing stardom. 'We didn't know if it would work. Lo and behold, it did.' It did indeed!

I don't know about you but I can't wait to see the true story of Lucky and Flo at the cinemas! What a great movie it would be.

 I believe in integrity. Dogs have it. Humans are sometimes lacking it.

CESAR MILLAN

NESBIT

Being a guide dog for the blind is not an easy job. But for Nesbit, there was one major perk to being George Kerscher's dog that made it all worthwhile... he got to see the world.

It's a dog's life sometimes when a family goes on holiday, or an extended foreign break, and are unable to pack their dog in a suitcase and take it on holiday with them. In fact, if you're a dog owner, most holidays begin with a tearful goodbye to your favourite pet outside of a dog hotel or hostel, or a friend's house.

In these days of pet passports and better travelling conditions for pets, journeying with dogs in particular is still a complicated and laborious process. Unless, that is, you're a guide dog. We all know that guide dogs get special treatment, and quite rightly so, but one dog in particular, a golden retriever called Nesbit, received some very fancy VIP treatment in his time as Kerscher's guide dog. In fact, Nesbit could lay claim, if he wanted to, to being the world's most travelled dog.

Now, I know there are hundreds of brilliant stories of dogs, like Bobbie the Wonder Dog (see chapter headed 'Bobbie'), who, against all the odds, travelled thousands of miles home after becoming stranded or lost from their families. And they are wonderful, heart-melting super stories, without a doubt. But, when it comes to distance travelled by plane, there are few other dogs in the world that have clocked up as many miles as Nesbit.

In his years as Kerscher's guide dog, Nesbit logged an astounding 1.2 million air miles with the American airline Delta. The reason behind this travelling odyssey is because Kerscher is a VIP, a man with an important globetrotting job. He is on the board of directors of Guide Dogs for the Blind, USA, and his job is to travel the world spreading the good work and achievements of this prestigious charity corporation. Kerscher is also dedicated to developing fully functional technology for the blind and visually impaired. Over the years that Nesbit worked and travelled alongside Kerscher, Delta thought it was only fair that Nesbit should be awarded his own frequent flier club card – the only dog in the world to have one – as well as the 1.2 million air miles. I like to think that when Nesbit retired – as he did in 2012 when Mikey, another golden retriever, took over his role – he packed up his doggy bag, got a taxi to the airport and booked a first-class round-the-world ticket, using his air miles, of course, and that he is now living a life of luxury plane-hopping between various exotic locations, sipping cocktails (Hair of the Dog, Salty Dog, etc) and poo-ing whenever, and wherever, he wants. Nesbit, we salute you!

 I would rather see the portrait of a dog that I know, than all the allegorical paintings they can show me in the world.

SAMUEL JOHNSON

TOBY

Every day, all around the world, a super dog saves somebody's life. And every day those stories are reported. Some are truly unexpected and unbelievable, and that's what makes them super indeed...

Dogs can jump, catch, fetch, learn words, be trained to help and protect blind people, detect cancer, sniff out bombs and even poo on command. You name it – DOGS CAN DO IT. But there are also some things that you wouldn't expect a dog to be able to do; things that seem to go against the laws of nature and science. After all these years of getting to know our furry best friends, they still have the ability to surprise us, or make us scratch our chins and wonder just what else can they do. There seems to be no end to their brilliance, and – from a scientific point of view – we are only still scratching the surface of their amazing capabilities.

So it should come as no surprise, but it will, to hear about the triumphant tale of Toby, the two-year-old golden retriever from Calvert, Maryland, USA, who defied all logic to keep calm and carry on, and magically save his owner's life – by giving her the Heimlich manoeuvre! Well, a doggy version of it!

Yep, you read that right!

This particular story, among the thousands that I read researching for this book, stands out. There was something about it that felt unique, as well as tickling me pink. Firstly, I won't lie, the visual image of a dog carrying out this lifesaving procedure made me curious, and secondly, I couldn't help wondering – as I am sure you are doing right now – just how on earth this super golden retriever did it?

In 2007, when the event took place, dog lover Debbie Parkhurst was taking a bite out of a lunchtime apple, as she had no doubt done thousands of times before, when suddenly, a small chunk of the fruit become lodged in her windpipe.

'It was lodged pretty tight,' she said, 'because I couldn't breathe. I tried to do the thing where you lean over a chair and give yourself the Heimlich, but it didn't work,' she continued. It was when she started beating her chest that Toby must have noticed something wrong was going on. 'The next thing I know,' she recalled, 'Toby's up on his hind feet and he's got his front paws on my shoulders. He pushed me to the ground, and once I was on my back, he began jumping up and down on my chest.'

This quick-thinking and decisive jumping by Toby managed to dislodge the apple from his owner's windpipe in the nick of time.

'As soon as I started breathing, he stopped and began licking my face, as if to keep me from passing out,' she said.

Amazing. Not only did Toby save his owner's life, he also provided some excellent quality aftercare. Soon after this traumatic experience, Parkhurst was driven to the doctor's by a friend – disappointingly, Toby did not do the driving – and was given the all clear.

'I literally have pawprint-shaped bruises on my chest,' she said at the time. 'Of all the dogs in the world, I never would have expected this goofy one here to know the Heimlich.'

Perhaps Toby, who had been rescued by the Parkhursts when he was found living in a local dumpster, had read the emergency measures recommended for choking victims by the American Heart Association and the American Red Cross. The protocol is to use a series of five hard thumps to the back, followed by a series of five abdominal thrusts. (This procedure, for your future safety reference, is known as the 'five and five'.) And while Toby's life-saving actions didn't precisely stick to these guidelines, his quick-thinking paw-jumps on Mrs Parkhurst's chest did the job in the nick of time.

At first, Parkhurst thought Toby believed that when she started choking she was wanting to play, but later she concluded that, in fact, once Toby knew she was in trouble, he knew what to do! 'I have no idea where he learned it from,' she recalled, when reporting the entire story to the local Maryland newspaper, the *Cecil Whig*. 'The doctor said I probably wouldn't be here without Toby,' she reported. For months after the event she kept remembering how lucky she was to be alive, but also how lucky she was to have Troy – her super dog: 'I keep looking at him and saying "You're amazing."' And I think I speak for all of us when I say, 'we think so too!'

Dogs love their friends and bite their enemies, quite unlike people, who are incapable of pure love and always have to mix love and hate.

SIGMUND FREUD

TROY

Dogs have a sense of smell a thousand times stronger than we have. Not only can they sniff out a three-day-old meatball that rolled under the sofa, they can also detect cancer in humans. Meet Troy – a super dog of lifesaving proportions.

Dogs have an incredible sense of smell. It's the first thing everybody learns about 'man's best friend' at school. Scientists have done sniffer-tests and concluded, after much nosing around, that dogs have a sense of smell far more powerful than humans, with an incredible 220 million smell (or olfactory, if you want to get technical) receptors in their konks. (Humans, by comparison, only have around five million of these receptors.) While most dogs demonstrate their acute sense of smell on a daily basis by nosing around the bin in the hope of licking packaging that once contained something that belonged to a cow or other tasty animal, some dog breeds can also use their Smell-o-Vision to startling, and lifesaving, effect.

Troy, a Doberman from New York, saved his owner Diane Papazian's life by being able to detect cancer in her breasts. She detailed how Troy 'nuzzled into her chest' when he was just a four-month-old puppy, so much so that she finally decided to see her doctor. It has long been thought that dogs can detect cancer cells in humans because cancer cells are known to produce chemicals called volatile organic compounds, which give off distinct odours that dogs are believed to react to. In fact, recent studies have shown that dogs can sniff out lung and breast cancer simply by smelling a patient's breath and urine samples.

Indeed, in January 2011, a study was released that detailed how a specially trained Labrador retriever named Marine was able to detect colorectal cancer 91 per cent of the time when sniffing patients' breath, and 97 per cent of the time when sniffing stools. When you think about it, it's pretty incredible that one dog's nose can do so much!

Anyway, Troy was able to smell these compounds in his owner, and by alerting her the only way he knew how – by nuzzling into her breast – he was able to show his concern. It was this constant nuzzling that brought about an itchy allergic reaction that, when scratched, showed up a visible lump which could also be felt. This lump was a tumour, undetected by a mammogram six months earlier. Papazian was diagnosed with aggressive breast cancer and went on to have a double mastectomy and chemotherapy. She is now, with a little help from her furry friend, cancer-free.

Word spread of Troy's amazing Early Detection System (sometimes known as a 'nose') and was subsequently nominated by the American Humane Association for the Hero Dog of the Year award 2013.

'I'm very grateful for Troy,' Papazian told the multitude of newspapers who reported the story, 'not only is he an amazing and compassionate dog, but he saved my life. During my recovery, having him around kept my mind occupied and he would just sit by me and look at me with his big brown eyes full of love.'

Troy, the dog that launched a thousand sniffs and saved his owner's life… by a nose.

 Every dog must have his day.

JONATHAN SWIFT

WHIZZ

Meet Whizz – the very cuddly Newfoundland giant that can rescue twelve people at once and swim faster than any human, considered the world's number one 'life-dog' and a very soft and cuddly 'living lifebelt'...

Life-dogs, like guide dogs, are truly one of mankind's greatest creations, where man and mutt meet and meld minds to become one: humans training dogs to become more like humans. It's amazing, isn't it?

Whizz – great name, great dog. Weighing in at an incredible 12 stone and standing proud at 6 feet tall on his mighty back legs ('Newfies' have incredibly large bones, which give them a much larger mass than your average dog), this incredible Newfoundland is a rescue dog born and bred to save lives.

Protecting the millions of Britons who descend upon the south coast of England for a jolly time on the ocean waves, Whizz the life-dog and his highly trained team of human lifeguards patrol up and down the coastline every day looking for stranded or 'in peril' seafarers, swimmers and boaters. To date, Whizz and his team have saved hundreds of lives by rescuing those in need in the treacherous, and often fatal, conditions that blast Britain's south coast.

The Newfoundland breed is specifically bred as a rescue dog. With their twice-as-thick waterproof fur, webbed feet, huge paw-span, intelligence and innate swimming ability, these beautiful beasts have the perfect build to help people out of dangerous water conditions.

And Whizz is no different – he is a gentle giant of a dog with a lifesaving CV as long and thick as his waterproof fur. The super-strength dog can haul up to twelve people (at once!) from the water, his huge paw-span aiding maximum propulsion and speed through the water. The breed's ability to swim has been described as a 'doggified version of breaststroke', though I like to think of it instead as a modified version of doggy paddle. Their unique swimming style crucially helps cut down the amount of time it takes to swim out to people in peril – a water-breed such as a Newfie has been recorded as swimming faster and longer than a human without suffering hypothermia in the UK's cold waters – and their massive lung capacity helps take in greater amounts of oxygen, vital to staying afloat for longer. Basically, think of Whizz as a big shaggy lifebuoy. That can swim. And lick you dry afterwards.

Known as the 'gentle giant' for his calm-under-pressure nature and rather docile nature when not scurrying around in the water, Whizz rose to fame as a local and national hero in 2007 when he plunged into an icy pool to save another dog from drowning. Since then, people from far and wide have travelled to Somerset, Whizz's home county, to shake his mega-paws and meet the dog in person, as it were. His owner, David Pugh, sums up what you must be thinking at this point: 'When you tell people a dog can rescue a dozen people, they don't believe you – that's why people come and see him.'

If you're interested in meeting Whizz, you should travel to the annual Bristol Harbourside Festival in July, where Whizz and the team demonstrate a forty-minute performance of their rescue skills to large, and always adoring, crowds.

 A dog has the soul of a philosopher.

PLATO

DOSHA

When Dosha woke up on 15 April 2003, no one could have imagined, or believed, the very bad day she was about to have. If she were a cat, she would be about to use up many of her nine lives...

Aged just ten months, a mere puppy, Dosha, a mixed-breed pit bull, ran out of her owner's home in Clearlake, California, USA, and onto the nearest road, where she was promptly run over by a car. Lying half dead at the side of the road – the victim of a hit and run – Dosha was left for (full) dead. Thankfully (in a way), the local police were called to the scene, but as Dosha was not wearing a collar her identity could not be immediately established. The police – believing Dosha to be fatally wounded – thought the most humane thing to do was to put the poor dog out of its misery and pain, and shoot it cleanly in the head. Officer Bob MacDonald unholstered his sidearm and, with sadness, shot Dosha just below her right eye. He then sealed her in a bag and drove to the nearest animal hospital, where the bag was placed in a freezer, its occupant considered dead. Very dead.

To everyone's complete surprise, not least the vet who had been made aware of the circumstances of this dog's very bad day, and who had gone to the freezer two hours later to check the body, Dosha was discovered very much alive and sitting upright inside the bag! The lucky-to-be-alive dog was treated immediately for hypothermia and a gunshot wound to the head, but – get this – no broken bones from the initial car accident. Dosha had survived her ordeal and was returned safely, and in full recovery mode, to her owner at the end of what turned out to be a very bad, but also a very good, day.

 You think dogs will not be in heaven? I tell you, they will be there long before any of us.

ROBERT LOUIS STEVENSON

OWNEY

Throughout modern history, dogs and postmen have never had a great relationship – dogs always eager to be the first to open the mail (even if it isn't theirs!) and postmen having spent well over a century scared by the overexcitable mutts that come to meet and greet them. However, Owney was different. Owney loved postmen – they were his friends and colleagues – but he also loved the smell of adventure too...

Born in 1887, Owney, a beautiful mixed-breed terrier, was a stray that was adopted as the first unofficial postal mascot by the Albany, New York, post office in 1888.

Owney the Postal Dog, as he was known, was for many years the world's most travelled dog, who instead of biting postmen worked alongside them, protecting their mail on long and winding train journeys! He was the guardian of railway mail, at the time a position of massive responsibility. Owney would bark and sneer if anyone other than a 'postie' tried to take the mail off a train!

Throughout his lifetime Owney travelled across all of the then forty-five states of America on the newly constructed railways, and even voyaged around the world to protect international mail in 1895. He travelled a total of over 140,000 miles by the time he was done! Owney was the first ever mascot of the

Railway Post Office and the United States Postal Service and his services to his country were commemorated in a 2011 US postage stamp that bore his proud and furry face!

 No man can be condemned for owning a dog. As long as he has a dog, he has a friend; and the poorer he gets, the better friend he has.

WILL ROGERS

SASHA

There are all sorts of detection dogs, whether used to find explosives or drugs, or to analyse the remnants of arson sites, or to track objects, humans or other animals. Meet Sasha – a super collie with a nose for trouble and for getting herself into 'deep water'...

For humans, breathing underwater is not possible without the aid of special apparatus, and, when it comes to sniffing underwater – being able to detect and differentiate different smells – humans rarely come up trumps. Smelling underwater is, quite simply, too difficult for the human body to manage, and for a long time scientists and biologists accordingly believed that most mammals could not smell underwater. Most do in fact usually just end up with lungs full of water, but Sasha, a beautiful black and white Border collie from Bolton, is different. She is Britain's first sniffer dog to become specifically trained to detect drowned or trapped bodies while submerged underwater. Yes, you read that correctly.

Sasha's unique nostrils are trained to detect the gaseous emissions emitted into the air by a decaying body at over 100 feet (30 metres) down. This, of course, has great practical implications for search and rescue teams all over the world where, immediately after a storm, flood or disaster-affected region – or while out at sea – Sasha is able to join the manhunt on board a boat and discover any traces of smells from any bodies trapped or submerged underwater, to a considerable depth.

Sasha, currently working for Bolton Mountain Rescue, has been named the country's first Drowned Victim Search Dog. Her training, which started when Sasha was just a seven-month-old pup with potential, required an intensive twelve-month programme, teaching Sasha how to use her nose and how to take advantage of her 220 million olfactory receptors.

Dog expert Neil Powell – working with Bolton Mountain Rescue – took this super dog under his wing, and made her take up the gauntlet of practical tests and field scenarios which, as Sasha's proud owner, Dave Marsh, admits, 'has never been done before anywhere in the world'.

In order to become a field agent, Sasha had to complete a series of 'sniff tests' to prove just how good her nose is when on the job. One of the sniff tests that she had to pass was to be able to smell a decaying body from 100 feet away. Of course, in her trials, Sasha's instructors were unable (much to their relief) to use a real dead human body. Instead, a dead pig was used – an animal that when dead emits a similar scent to humans. The dead pig, which was submerged and hidden underwater twenty-four hours before Sasha's trial, was the bait. Then Sasha and her team were taken on a boat to see if Sasha would pick up on the scent and start barking to indicate that they were close. She did.

After her intense training, Sasha is now a proud member of the Bolton Mountain Rescue team, and the work completed by Neil Powell and her master Dave Marsh is further evidence of how continuing research into the abilities of detection dogs can further aid their human counterparts and increase the efficiency of search and rescue operations.

 The dog represents all that is best in man.

ETIENNE CHARLET

RUPEE

While reports of this super dog's achievements may have been exaggerated in the press, make no mistake, the feat recorded by Rupee was truly superheroic. Rupee's climb to the top proved that, even for dogs, the impossible is possible...

Nicknamed the 'slumdog' in the world's press, Rupee, a dog more used to climbing piles of rubbish in landfill slums as a homeless stray, finally had his day in the spotlight. And what a day it was. Rupee became the first ever dog on record to climb to Mount Everest's iconic base camp. But with the world's media making a dog's dinner of Rupee's astonishing feat back in November 2013, the dog-hungry public became confused about what Rupee had actually achieved. The world's TV and newspaper press went bananas over the story but, as so often happens, got the truth wrong. Had Rupee been the first dog to climb Mount Everest all the way to the top like all the TV presenters and newspapers claimed he had?

No. Rupee had not climbed the 29,029 feet (8,848 metres) up to the top of the world's highest mountain. No dog has ever done that. And, I'm sorry to report, it's highly unlikely any dog could on its own. Not even a super dog like Rupee. However, he was the first dog to reach the height of 17,598 feet (5,364 metres) above sea level; over halfway to the top of the mountain's peak. It might not be as 'sexy' as making it to the top of Everest, but that doesn't matter – Rupee's ascent to base camp is even more remarkable considering how close he had been to rock bottom. But it was at his lowest point, in the literal gutter, that Rupee found his shining star, Joanne Lefson – a worldwide Internet sensation.

When Lefson found Rupee down in the dumps, she had already found fame on the Internet with her previous dog, Oscar, known on thousands of websites and blogs as the 'globetrotting dog' on account of their epic adventures around the world together. Lefson famously posted images of Oscar at some of the world's most exotic locations, including while hot air ballooning in Cape Town, helicoptering through the Grand Canyon, and on top of the Eiffel Tower, to name but three. Oscar and Lefson's global expedition was not, however, a flight of fancy. Not at all. Their travels to some of the farthest corners of the earth was to highlight the plight of the estimated half a billion shelter dogs currently without a home all over the globe, and their adventures saw the dognamic duo visit over 20,000 dog shelters along the way.

They had journeyed across five continents and made the headlines everywhere they went, their trip being reported in every new city they visited. They were on a mission. Lefson claimed that she would not stop travelling and raising awareness for stray dogs until 'every dog had a home'. And she meant it. She sold her house and everything she owned so she could travel the world speaking on behalf of homeless, abandoned dogs without a voice. Dogs that had been left to die.

Sadly, however, Lefson's beloved Oscar was killed in a car accident in January 2013, before they could finish their task together. Lefson was distraught. How could she carry on?

But then, how could she not carry on? Too much good work had been done!

Rather than give up her cause, and see all of her (and Oscar's) dreams fade away unrealised, Lefson decided that Oscar's legacy was for her to continue bravely without him. It was her duty to pick herself up, dust herself off and find a new partner-in-flight, a dog with whom she could continue all of her charitable work, a dog that would be her new travelling companion to experience new sights and smells, a dog that would help touch and inspire the lives of millions of people (and dogs).

And so it was, on her search high and low for her next companion, that she found her new inspiration – Rupee.

She discovered Rupee at a slum – literally on top of a massive pile of rubbish – in Ladakh, north India. Rupee was a homeless dog, living on and off the streets, half-dead through starvation and dehydration. Nobody loved him. Nobody wanted to love him. 'When I saw him on that dumpsite he couldn't have had more than an hour to live,' Lefson said. 'He couldn't even walk ten metres without collapsing.' And Rupee was just the dog she was looking for.

Lefson saw something in Rupee, a fighting spirit that she herself had refused to abandon. She picked Rupee up, dusted him off, and vowed to make him happy and healthy.

In preparation for the expeditions to follow, and to get him fighting fit once again, Lefson fed Rupee a high-protein diet of boiled eggs and rice, and he was in tip-top condition (not to mention the brand new owner of a shiny new sweet-smelling coat to replace his old tattered fur) when Lefson departed to continue her travels with her new companion. And it was to be her biggest challenge to date. The trek to Everest's base camp took ten long days. For even a trained mountaineer, getting to base camp on foot is no walk in the park; it is a gruelling craggy trek full of dangers and potentially fatal weather conditions.

When you consider that Rupee was so close to death, abandoned, unloved and simply too poorly to put one paw in front of the other, and then climbed halfway up the highest peak on earth, well, it just makes me smile as wide as Mount Everest itself. I wonder where Lefson and Rupee will go next?

 All knowledge, the totality of all questions and all answers is contained in the dog.

KAFKA

TRAKR

Out of tragedy sometimes comes triumph. And out of the wreckage of one of modern history's most terrible terrorist attacks, comes Trakr, considered by Time magazine to be the 'most heroic animal of all time'.

Trakr was one of the most honoured police dogs in Canadian police history, having helped seize over $1 million worth of drugs and put dozens of criminals behind bars. With his service to his country complete, the German shepherd retired from the Halifax Police Force and settled down peacefully to live out his days playing 'fetch' in the park with his master, James Symington, and to eat all the sausages he could manage. That is, until 11 September 2001.

After seeing search and rescue operations in the aftermath of the terrorist strike in New York City on his television, Symington drove with Trakr for fifteen hours from Prospect Bay, Nova Scotia to Manhattan, to what was to become known as Ground Zero. He was determined to help locate and rescue any survivors. Arriving on the morning of 12 September, Trakr found a sign of life under the rubble, the last survivor of 9/11 – Genelle Guzman. Genelle had been on the thirteenth floor of the South Tower when it collapsed and had been trapped for over twenty-four hours in the burning remains. Just as all hope had begun to fade, Genelle was found by Trakr.

Trakr was a hero. A doggy hero.

But this story of an amazing super dog doesn't end there. There's more. Much more.

On 14 September, two days after his heroic find among the smouldering rubble, Trakr collapsed from chemical and smoke inhalation. People feared the worst. Was Trakr to become another victim of 9/11? No, he wasn't. Coaxed back from the brink of his dreadful ordeal, he lived to see another day.

After eight years of retirement, Trakr was living happily back in Halifax, a local and national hero – and now an old dog indeed – when his old pal Symington, after reading an essay by a local cloning company, entered him into a competition to find the world's most 'clone-worthy' dog, believing Trakr had everything that was required to win. He was right. Out of a list of 200 applicants, Trakr's DNA was considered the best. Trakr's instincts and bravery at the World Trade Centre all those years earlier had reminded the panel of judges just how super he was: he was an obvious choice, a dog that deserved to have his DNA passed down for future generations. In 2009, five cloned puppies were produced from his exceptional DNA. They are called Trust, Solace, Valor, Prodigy, and Déjà Vu and are alive and well and following in their father's hefty pawprints. Sadly, Trakr never got to meet his cloned offspring, though I'm sure he would have been a proud father.

Trakr died in April 2009, at the grand old age of fourteen, due to a neurological condition called degenerative myelopathy, which his vet attributed to inhaling large volumes of smoke during the events of 9/11. Before he died, and due to his illness, he lost movement in his hind legs and they had to be removed. His loyal pal, Symington, acquired a dog-cart so Trakr could power himself around with his front paws – continued proof that this special old dog was super-strong to the end. A true American hero, a true super dog.*

 The greatest fear dogs know is the fear that you will not come back when you go out the door without them.

STANLEY COREN

---

* If you want to read another story of a search and rescue dog that helped save lives in the wake of 9/11, I suggest you read the heartbreaking tale of Sirius. This beautiful dog was attached to the Port Authority Police Department, New York, and was the only dog to lose his life while trying to save people amongst the rubble. It's not a story with a happy ending, but it is a story of a super dog that will make you appreciate how amazing these incredibly trained dogs are.

ROSELLE

For Michael Hinson, the incredible calmness displayed by one very special dog on 11 September 2001 would change his life in a most unexpected way...

Roselle, like Trakr (and over two hundred other rescue dogs), was a super dog whose 'superness' arose from the rubble of tragedy on 9/11. No human or dog deserves to encounter a devastating event of such magnitude, but to survive it is nothing short of a miracle.

In order to tell the story of Roselle's unbelievable calm under pressure, we have to go back to 9 a.m. on that fateful morning. It was a beautifully sunny day and Roselle, like she did every day, was taking a well-deserved nap under the desk of her owner, computer salesman Hinson, on the seventy-eighth floor of Tower One, World Trade Centre. Hinson, blind from birth, loved and relied on Roselle for his life. As today was about to prove.

Roselle, a classic yellow Labrador retriever, was sharply awoken from her slumber when the first plane, Flight 11, impacted into the tower fifteen floors above them. With chaos soon engulfing the entire building, Roselle – on the directions from Hinson that they needed to leave urgently – calmly led her blind friend over to stairwell B, and then began the long journey down 1,463 steps out of the tower. Roselle's training in an emergency had kicked in.

As they descended down the dark, smoky, cramped and increasingly panic-ridden stairwell, she led Hinson (as well as thirty other trapped people, it later transpired) on the hour-long descent to safety. Within mere moments of them exiting the tower, it collapsed. Hinson later announced to local newspapers that, 'While everyone ran in panic, Roselle remained totally focused on her job. While debris fell around us, and even hit us, Roselle stayed calm.' She then led Hinson to safety near to a local subway station and away from the falling debris and smoke clouds that covered the entire lower half of Manhattan in white powder. She had saved her friend and owner by guiding him down seventy-eight floors of mayhem and chaos.

Hinson stated that, that afternoon when Roselle and he arrived home, she immediately began playing with Hinson's retired guide dog, Linnie, Roselle's predecessor, and carried on as if what had happened earlier that very day was no biggie; she was just doing her job like she was trained to do.

Hinson was so inspired by the courage under fire and loyalty displayed by the dog that saved his life, he quit his job as a computer salesman and became Public Affairs Officer for Guide Dogs for the Blind.[*]

 Qui me amat, amet et canem meum.
(Love me, love my dog.)

ST BERNARD

---

[*] Roselle died in 2011, aged thirteen. She was posthumously named American Hero Dog of the Year by the American Humane Society.

TREO

Treo was a naughty dog. So naughty that his former owners sent him packing to the army, hoping the discipline and training would turn him into a good dog. They were right. Treo the Bomb Sniffer Dog is now the most decorated dog in the British Army.

One of twenty-five expertly trained explosives dogs deployed in Afghanistan in 2008, and a member of the 104 Military Working Dog Support Unit (part of the Royal Army Veterinary Corps), Treo, a black Labrador retriever, had a gift for sniffing out bombs or, put another way, a nose for saving lives. Treo and his handler, Dave Heyhoe – known to his fellow soldiers as 'the dog whisperer' – became inseparable while on their tours in Afghanistan, and together they became so important that many soldiers refused to patrol certain areas without being accompanied by them.

On 1 August 2008, while stationed in Helmand Province – a notorious location for bombs and Taliban insurgents, and one of the danger hotspots known to all soldiers – Treo sniffed out an improvised explosive device, known as an IED (or bark-bark-bark, in dog). This particular type of IED was also referred to as a 'daisy chain' because of the way multiple explosive devices were wired together and hidden out of sight on roads that the soldiers were known to patrol. A month later, Treo sniffed out another daisy chain.

By having such a sensitive nose, Treo saved the lives of dozens of British soldiers as well as civilians. He was awarded the Dickin Medal, the highest military honour an animal can receive, and tried his very best not to bury it in the back garden when he returned home to London with his new best friend, and now owner, Heyhoe. Heyhoe was so grateful of the bond he experienced with Treo in Afghanistan, that he wrote a book about him, *It's All About Treo*, in 2012. The things Heyhoe and his soldier colleagues (human and canine) achieved, which are detailed brilliantly in the book, is enough to make any civilian think they're barking mad! But they're not, they're just super-soldiers risking their lives to do a super job.

From troublemaker to lifesaver, it's dogs like Treo that make you realise there are some creatures in this world that were just born to sniff out danger.

If you don't have a dog there may not be something wrong with you, but there may be something wrong with your life.

VINCENT VAN GOGH

RECORD-
BREAKING
SUPER DOGS

Every day a newspaper or website announces
that a new world record has been set. But there
are no world records anywhere on planet earth
that are as entertaining as those achieved by
super dogs. Here are some of the best...

ABELLATINO ARABELLA (TIA, FOR SHORT)

Pop, pop, pop, pop, pop, pop, pop, pop, pop, pop, pop, pop, pop, pop, pop, pop, pop, pop, pop, pop, pop, pop, pop, pop... that is the sound that was made by Tia, the proud, but no doubt exhausted, doggy mum of the largest litter of puppies ever. We salute you, supermum!

In 2009, when American Nadya Suleman gave birth to eight babies (in one sitting), she became a global sensation and was immediately dubbed 'Octomum' by the world's press. But let's skip back to a few years before Nadya's biggest release to 2004, 29 November to be precise, when Tia, a doggy supermum, gave birth to the largest litter of puppies ever recorded.

Tia gave birth to twenty-four puppies – twenty-four tiny Neapolitan mastiffs – almost double the amount of pups that is usually littered by this particular breed. When news spread of this beautiful achievement, local, national and international media camped out on the front lawn of the breeders, Damien Ward and Anne Kellegher, in Cambridgeshire, to report the story that was to melt a million dog lovers' hearts.

Sadly, of the twenty-four brand new puppies born by Caesarean section, one was stillborn and three died in the first week. Thankfully, though, the other twenty pups were OK and survived their first-of-a-kind ordeal. Of the twenty-four pups delivered, nine were female and fifteen were male and, when fully grown, could potentially weigh up to 13 stone each and be over two foot tall. A handful, for sure!

Two-year-old Tia survived the very long birth, and had just enough energy afterwards to give the dogfather, appropriately called Caesar given the nature of the birth, a good telling off. 'It's all your fault, you did this to me!' Tia could be heard barking loudly throughout the maternity ward. The previous Guinness World Record for the largest litter was twenty-three.

 The world was conquered through the understanding of dogs; the world exists through the understanding of dogs.

FRIEDRICH NIETZSCHE

BIG SPLASH

Owning a dog can be very expensive – dog food ain't cheap. But when it comes to massive price tags, Big Splash takes the biscuit...

Ladies and gentlemen, may I introduce you to the world's most expensive dog... Big Splash! For those of you with fancy tastes, this story of a beautiful, red Tibetan mastiff will delight your mind... and burn a hole in your back pocket. In March 2011, Big Splash became the world's priciest dog – a super dog indeed – when he was sold by breeder Lu Liang to a Chinese multimillionaire coal baron for ten million Chinese yuan. That's a fur-raising £945,000!

Now, to be fair, Tibetan mastiffs are rather large, so the new owner definitely got his money's worth in that sense; Big Splash weighed 180 lbs (13 stone, or 63 kilos) at the time of the sale so, pound for pound, Big Splash is worth £6,750 per lb, which isn't quite so bad, I suppose. We should perhaps just enjoy the irony of an expensive dog being called Big Splash. (Translated back into Chinese, this beautiful red beast is known as Hong Dong.)

Red Tibetan mastiffs are an absolutely glorious breed of dog, not to mention a burgeoning status symbol for rich and powerful Chinese. Sometimes referred to as 'the closest thing to a lion you can legally own', these beguilingly huge and fluffy creatures are also considered holy animals, with many Tibetans believing them to have the souls of monks and nuns who were not reincarnated as humans last time round, i.e. because they were 'promoted' to Tibetan mastiffs. No matter what you believe spiritually, these beautiful red dogs seem to me to be worth every yuan.

According to the breeder, Big Splash is a 'perfect specimen' whose price tag is justified; Queen Victoria and Marco Polo would no doubt have agreed, as both owned Tibetan mastiffs in their time, with the latter describing them as 'tall as a donkey with a voice as powerful as that of a lion'.

If you have the cash to splash, Tibetan mastiffs are a perfect choice of loyal protector against intruders *and* massive fluffy pillow all rolled into one. Big Splash is reported to enjoy a diet of gourmet chicken and beef (perhaps sprinkled with ground-up diamonds?) to the tune of £100,000 a year! Lucky dog, indeed! So, if you're thinking of feeding your newly acquired and very expensive Tibetan mastiff with plain ol' tinned dog food, expect them to turn their rather snooty noses up at it!

 You will be amazed to find that almost all an Englishman's pleasures can be... shared by his dog.

GEORGE BERNARD SHAW

MAX

Here lies Max,
the world's
oldest super dog.
Doggone, but
not forgotten...

Part beagle, part dachshund and part terrier, Max was a true pick 'n' mix of a mutt that can – to this day – claim to have been the oldest dog in the world. Max lived to the very grand old age of 29 years 282 days and remains the champion of dog years.

Max's roots were tied (via his leash) to an American sugarcane farmer from Louisiana, who gave him up for adoption in 1983. Thankfully, his new owner, Janelle Derouen, loved Max to the max and gave him a wonderful home for all his long years.

However, it wasn't until 15 May 2013 that *Guinness World Records* certified Max to be the oldest dog on the planet, making him very famous indeed. Regrettably, being crowned the world's oldest dog was also something of a bad luck omen as, tragically, Max died three days after being awarded the honour. As with many old dogs, he died of a grand mal seizure, but had he lived for just another three months, he would have been the first known dog to reach thirty years of age. Life can be so cruel...

Twenty-nine human years works out in dog years to be around 203, although the age-old maxim of a dog-year equalling seven human years is no longer considered accurate. And with Max being a very mixed breed, it's difficult to tell just how old he was in dog-years. However, what is known, and what was celebrated by all those people who travelled from around the world to shake Max's paw after his award, is that good ol' Max more than doubled his breed's life expectancy.

 Thou call'st me dog before thou hadst a cause, But since I am a dog, beware my fangs.

WILLIAM SHAKESPEARE

OBIE

Recent research shows that, in the UK alone, approximately 35 per cent of all dogs are overweight. It's an expanding problem. However, one story shines a light on how, with a lot of love (and a few less treats), our super dogs can find healthiness as well as happiness...

Obie is a big-boned dog, and for a while he was a very chubby one. Gloriously large in bulk and spirit, his chubbiness was adorable, but there were of course inverse health effects to consider. In August 2012, Obie weighed a dangerously unhealthy 77 lbs – that's 5.5 stone (or 35 kilos) of pure sausage. Something had to change.

Originating from Portland, Oregon, USA, Obie was a sausage dog with a hot dog of a problem – he looked more like a sausage than he did a dog*. In fact, Obie was so fat he was dubbed the world's fattest dog.

With dog obesity a growing problem all over the world, it's an issue that dog owners who like to treat their pets every day should be aware of, especially the long-term damage to the dog's health, which may include diabetes, heart disease or arthritis. It can also be difficult to secure pet insurance for an obese dog.

* If you feel your doggy may be a bit of a meaty monster, then you should check out the 'Dog Size-o-Meter' on the PFMA (Pet Food Manufacturers Association) website.

But don't worry… Obie is currently on a lifesaving diet to shed his puppy fat and achieve a healthy weight, an average dachshund weight, which is around 30-40 lbs (14-18 kilos).

Obie's elderly former owners had plied their adorable dog with too many daily treats, causing his weight to balloon to bursting proportions, but in little over a year, between 2012 and 2013, Obie – with the help of his new owner, Nora Vanatta, obviously – has transformed himself from 77 lbs of rich sausage meat to a very trim, healthy and happy 30 lb medium-sized hot dog (without the bun).

During Obie's intense weight-loss programme, Vanatta decided to set up a website to chronicle his progress and thereby update visitors to the site (of which there became many hundreds of thousands!) who wanted to be kept in the loop about Obie's progress. You can still follow his weight loss online at www.obiedog.com (the pictures of Obie's weight loss are dramatic when viewed retrospectively), but I can happily report that, after surgery to remove 2.5 lbs of loose skin, Obie is looking rather dashing. He is also dashing about on an interstate tour across the USA, appearing on nationwide daytime TV programmes and meeting and greeting the thousands of fans who have followed his journey from sausage roll to hot dog.

 Why do dachshunds wear their ears inside out?

P. G. WODEHOUSE

FREDDY

Freddy the Great Dane is 7 ft 1 in (2.16 m) tall and weighs 18 stone (114 kilos). In 2014, he was hailed as the 'tallest dog in Britain'. A true super dog...

Dogs – and in particular, super dogs – come in all shapes and sizes, colours and breeds and, of course, smells. But, of course, the area of super dogs that often attracts most people's attention is their size. And, my word, Freddy is HUGE!

What is even more amazing is that this giant dog has not yet reached maturity and *is therefore still growing*. At the moment, we can only take bets on how big he'll end up. Freddy – at the time of writing – is still only eighteen months old, which means that by the time he's three years old he'll be the size of a house! OK, maybe not that big, but certainly a contender for the crown of 'world's tallest dog'.

The tallest dog in the world currently, according to the people with the measuring tape at *Guinness World Records*, is Zeus, a four-year-old Great Dane from Michigan, USA, who is 7 ft 4 in (2.24 m) tall when standing on hind legs. Zeus is a mega-dog, because that's the same size as many a horse! But will Freddy outgrow him? Freddy's rightfully proud owner Claire Stoneman (5 ft 4 in), from Leigh-on-Sea, Essex, spends £4,000 on feeding her Freddy every year and is, no doubt, too afraid to play 'fetch' with him in case he bowls her over or brings back a stick twice the size of her.

If Freddy does grow to become the world's tallest dog, as many believe he will, he will be showered with praise and love just as Zeus is. Zeus's fame takes him all around the world; even 'writing' his own book and appearing on many major daytime TV shows. Freddy is already being coveted by the world's media, who are, with frenzied excitement, waiting expectantly for Freddy to overtake Zeus's height.

Let's all keep an eye out for Freddy in the coming months to see if he grows up just the right amount – from underdog to the world's tallest super dog...

 What do dogs do on their day off? Can't lie around – that's their job!

GEORGE CARLIN

MILLY

Let's take a quick peek inside the life of the 'world's smallest dog', Milly – a super teenie tiny dog that's making big headlines!

As of the first few months of 2014 (the Year of the Horse, not Dog, sadly – according to the Chinese zodiac calendar), the world's smallest dog is Milly: a chihuahua from Puerto Rico, measuring a very dainty 3.8 inches (9.65 cm) high – that's over 6 feet (1.83 m) smaller than Freddy the Great Dane!

For the thousands of her fans, Milly is a super dog and a true miracle of nature, *just by being born*, let alone surviving and thriving.

Back in December 2011, news of Milly's birth quickly spread around her local town of Dorado, Puerto Rico. She was so small she could fit on a teaspoon and had to be fed with an eye dropper... and she weighed just one solitary pound (450 grams)! Within days, fascinated dog lovers all over Puerto Rico were flocking like sheep to catch a glimpse of this mini-mutt, a dog that would soon become a national celebrity and worldwide sensation, with over 300,000 followers on Facebook under the moniker 'Miracle Milly'. In 2013, Milly's website (www.miraclemilly.com) took off and proudly claimed, 'She may be tiny but Milly's on the verge of something big – being officially recognised as the most petite pooch on the planet.'

Milly's very pink and fluffy website is home to many of Milly's mini adventures; you can watch videos of Milly's travels around the world as well as her local and international TV interviews (very funny!) You can even buy from the Miracle Milly Collection clothing line, which boasts a veritable feast of doggy dresses in bright neon colours.

Milly, who had taken the smallest dog crown from the previous world title-holder Boo Boo, another female chihuahua (from Kentucky, USA), sleeps in a baby's crib and is so small that she still fits snugly into the palm of a hand at the age of three. Her owner, Vanessa Semler, proudly declares that when people come to visit Milly to take photos, she has a habit of sticking out her tongue. 'She knows how to pose,' Semler says.

The breeding of super-tiny dogs – sometimes known as 'Hollywood chihuahuas' – is an increasingly popular area of pet-keeping, with many mini-dogs being bred to be as small as possible. Celebrity socialite, Paris Hilton, is a famous example of a superstar who carries her dog, Tinkerbell, around in her clutch bag wherever she goes.

Chihuahuas, one of the world's smallest breed of dogs, usually reach a height of between 6 and 10 inches (15–25 cm), so at just 3.8 inches (9.65 cm), Milly is super-super-*super* small.

 A dog teaches a boy fidelity, perseverance, and to turn around three times before lying down.

ROBERT BENCHLEY

SUPER DOGS OF MYTH AND FICTION

Every culture has a mythological dog story, with lessons
for us to learn and pass on for future generations. Some
stories tell of super dogs who achieved fantastical feats,
or displayed great loyalty and honour in the face of
adversity; others tell of beasts sent from down below to
terrorise and prophesise; while yet others are created
from the minds of men to be but mirrors, reflecting how
we see ourselves and how we also view the world.

ARGOS

You may not be familiar with the legend of Argos, but it is a truly epic story of one super dog's love and loyalty for his master that has been retold for over 3,000 years.

The *Odyssey* is an epic poem, commonly attributed to Homer. It is one of the oldest surviving pieces of western literature, a poem that influenced much of what came after it. I won't pretend I've read it, not even the translated English version of it, but I do know that within the 12,000-line-long poem we can find an amazing, if very simple, super dog story that has survived and thrived for many generations: the legend of Argos.

After twenty years of desperately trying to return to his home city of Ithaca, the Greek king Odysseus finally arrives at the borders of his homeland. Upon entering the gates leading up to his home, his Great Hall, he realises that his once stately pile has been taken over by thugs, keen to take Odysseus's wife, Penelope, as their own slave.

Quickly disguising himself as a beggar, Odysseus begins the long walk up to the Great Hall, where suddenly he spots his old friend, his once-brave and heroic dog, Argos. The formerly proud and powerful dog, now abandoned, has been reduced to a mangy mutt just about holding on to life.

Abandoned for two decades in Odysseus's absence, Argos had been left to die on the side of the road, unloved and unwanted. His dog-bed, once made of the finest cottons, was now nothing more than a pile of cow manure. Argos had only one reason to live: his loyalty, and it was this loyal love of his old master that had kept him going.

As Odysseus walks past his old friend – after twenty years of not seeing one another – Argos looks up at the apparent stranger, and despite his weakness and ill health, immediately recognises him. Odysseus is not dead, but alive, and back to reclaim his house, his land and his throne. Not wanting to expose his disguise, Odysseus is unable to greet his dog after all this time, but Argos knows this and simply wags his tail and drops his ears, just enough to let his master know that he recognises him. And then, peacefully, and comforted by having seen his master alive once more, Argos dies knowing that Odysseus will – after years of war and being away from home – reclaim what is rightfully his.

Did You Know?

The record amount of knots undone by a dog in three minutes is fourteen. Achieved by Ben, a Japanese spaniel owned by Claudia Neumann, at the Vienna Recordia event in Austria on 26 September 2010. After he achieved the feat, Ben casually handed the pieces of untied rope to his owner.

LADY AND THE TRAMP

The classic dog-love-story that transcends generations, *Lady and the Tramp* was Walt Disney's first animated feature to be filmed in widescreen Cinemascope, as well as the first full-length cartoon that was based on an original story.

Rich girl meets poor boy. Poor boy's attempts to woo rich girl are clumsy. Rich girl falls for poor boy's charms. Boy and girl have hilarious socio-economic and cultural issues. Boy and girl eat spaghetti. Boy and girl fall in love. Girl gets kidnapped. Boy rescues girl. Girl and boy move in together and live happily ever after.

In a nutshell, that's the plot of the classic *Lady and the Tramp*, the first animated love story between two dogs ever to be seen on screen. Not only one of the best doggy-duo films ever made, it also proved that spaghetti with meatballs isn't such a bad choice of meal for a romantic night out, especially if your intentions are impure.

Lady and the Tramp was first released in 1955 and was the first Disney movie that was based on an original story, a distinct departure from the Mickey Mouse Club features of the time (Ward Greene wrote the screenplay based on his own book, *Happy Dan, the Whistling Dog*). The gamble not only paid off, but also laid the foundation for a wealth of new stories and characters to be developed. In 2011, *Time* magazine voted the film one of the '25 All Time Best Animated Films'.

Did You Know?

Twenty-two per cent of people actually mix up their dog's name with their partner's.

GUINEFORT

Throughout history a great many people have been awarded the prestigious title of 'Saint'. But, so far at least, only one dog has ever received that blessing.

In the thirteenth century, so the legend goes, a French knight from Lyon left his infant son in the paws of his trusted and faithful greyhound, Guinefort, for the day. Perhaps not the best parenting decision ever made, but I like the fact that he felt Guinefort could handle the responsibility of looking after a child.

Anyway, upon returning home from a long day of duelling, jousting and general knighting, the warrior found his home torn apart, blood smeared all across Guinefort's face, and his young son nowhere to be seen. Thinking his loyal dog had eaten the child, the knight instantly shot him dead with an arrow. Then, seconds later, in typical child fashion (never to be found when needed!), his son walked into the room, alive, and holding the remains of a mutilated snake.

The knight, distraught at having impulsively killed the family pet without learning all the facts, was so upset by his trigger-happiness that he buried Guinefort in a well near the house and erected a shrine on top of it in the dog's honour. Guinefort, after all, was a hero – he had protected the knight's son by killing the snake. A saintly act, deserving saintly recognition.

Local villagers, who heard of the incident, prayed for the dog and, as the myth and legend grew, many desperate people even left their sick and dying babies at Guinefort's burial site, believing the dog to be a saintly protector of infants. And that is how Guinefort the Brave, a dog who was wrongfully killed for doing the right thing, became Guinefort, Saint of Infants. Perhaps this tale carries a dog-tastic moral for us all to remember in the heat of the moment: impulse and impatience can kill.

Did You Know?

The world record for the most tennis balls held in a dog's mouth at one time is five. Augie, a golden retriever owned by the Miller family of Dallas, Texas, USA, successfully held all five balls in its mouth on 6 July 2003.

KRYPTO

Superman's dog. Yes, Superman had a pet dog! Called Krypto the Superdog. Is it a bird? Is it a plane? No, it's a dog! A super dog!

Krypto the Superdog. A fictional super dog, yes, but still a super dog! And the only alien (i.e. not from earth) super dog to be included in this book. So that makes Krypto even more super than he already is.

Krypto is Superman's pet dog, created by the legendary comic book publisher, DC, the creator of all the Superman comics since the red-and-blue-clad character's first appearance in 1938. You'll no doubt be familiar with the legend of Superman, but what do you know of his dog?

Krypto first appeared in the now iconic comic adventures of Superboy in 1955. Krypto's precise breed is never mentioned in any of the comics, and his appearance has altered over the past fifty years, from powerful dog with incredible responsibility to child-friendly cartoon dog with its tongue constantly hanging out. Krypto is simply drawn as a generic white dog with a cape, possibly a Labrador retriever, but thankfully not a pug or chihuahua.

Originally the pet dog of Kal-El (Superman's birth name while he was a child on Krypton), Krypto was the trusted friend and loyal dog of the El family. However, in need of a test pilot for one of his new rocket ships, Superman's dad, Jor-El, sent Krypto out into the cold expanses of space. Krypto's rocket ship got knocked off course and, somewhat conveniently, landed billions of light years away on earth – Superman's future home when Kal-El himself arrived here from an imploding Krypton. Kal-El (as Clark Kent) would later be reunited with Krypto as a young boy living on earth.

Krypto's character has endured beyond his original role and still survives as a very popular children's cartoon character.

So, you're probably wondering what made Krypto so super. Well, let me tell you…

- Super strength, speed, durability, and stamina.
- Flight – a flying dog!
- Physical invulnerability.
- Super-breath, including freeze-breath expelled through his bark!
- Super-hearing.
- Super-vision powers – including X-ray vision, heat vision, telescopic vision, and microscopic vision.
- Acute sensory powers – including the ability to see, hear and feel the entire electromagnetic spectrum!
- Good snuggler and wonderful companion.

I made the last one up, but no super-powered dog can be called a super dog without the ability to snuggle and keep their owner's feet warm, and the thought of Superman and Krypto going for walkies through the air together, or of Superman having to poop-a-scoop Krypto's doggy-do in mid air, is almost too funny to think of!

Did You Know?

In 2012, Battersea Dogs and Cats Home reunited 962 lost dogs with their owners.

BLACK SHUCK

Black Shuck – a mythological hell-hound, a demon ghost dog, believed to haunt the ancient roads of Suffolk, England. As legend goes, Black Shuck is also the inspiration for Sir Arthur Conan Doyle's *The Hound of the Baskervilles*. Read on... but beware of the dog!

Black Shuck is a dog the size of a cow, with blazing red eyes and the darkest of dark black fur. Although some reports also say he is the size of a horse, and other sightings suggest he is no larger than a big dog, it is commonly believed, whatever his size, that he is as evil as the most evil demon from Hell.

Whatever you may have heard about Black Shuck's appearance, the mythology behind this supernatural hell-hound is that he was left behind by his Viking master in AD 787, has terrified the Suffolk coast for centuries, and is apparently still alive and terrorising the local residents today.

According to local legend, Black Shuck prowls along dark country lanes and lonesome footpaths, where, 'although his howling makes the hearer's blood run cold, his footfalls make no sound'. According to the 'eye-witness' account of Reverend Abraham Fleming, the two most 'accurate' sightings of Black Shuck happened on the same day in August 1577, and both happened in churches. On that day a massive lightning storm was raging along the Suffolk Coast, and the townsfolk of Bungay, a local village, had congregated at the nearby St Mary's church (still there to this day) to pray for their lives. Suddenly, a snap of lightning from above crashed the church doors wide open. It was Black Shuck.

The demon-dog galloped through the praying congregation and 'wrung the necks' of a man and a boy who were on their knees praying, leaving the rest of the churchgoers as witnesses of his terrible power. Then, as quickly as he arrived, he disappeared. He stomped his feet and the church steeple fell crashing through the roof, but left enough space for Black Shuck to blast his fiery way out of the church, leaving scorch marks on the door that can still be seen to this day. Ever since then the mystery and mythology surrounding the appearances of Black Shuck have infiltrated popular culture and the legend lives on. Indeed, it was the sightings of Black Shuck that inspired Sir Arthur Conan Doyle's legendary tale of his very own furry beast in *The Hound of the Baskervilles*, a book that was published 300 years after Black Shuck's church visit. Doyle took elements of the Black Shuck myth and relocated them to Dartmoor in Devon, where he let his own demon-dog run amuck amongst the wealthy Baskerville family. The question is: will we ever see Black Shuck again?*

Life is like a dog sled team. If you ain't the lead dog, the scenery never changes.

LEWIS GRIZZARD

* There are other mythological dog stories that are told and retold throughout the British Isles, such as the benevolent Gytrash (a beast that wanders northern England looking to lead lost travellers back to the right path), the dastardly Barghast (a demon-dog local to Yorkshire), and Gwyllgi, 'The Dog of Darkness' (a ghostly mastiff that terrifies the Welsh valleys with its blazing red eyes).

SWEEP

Sweep, Sooty's silly sidekick and lover of bones and sausages, is the most enduring doggy puppet of all time. Indeed, the Sooty Show is officially recognised by Guinness World Records as the longest-running children's programme of all time.

When I was eight my parents took me to see the *Travelling Sooty Show* at the Northcroft Leisure Centre in Newbury, Berkshire. This was the mid 1980s, when puppet shows at leisure centres were all the rage, and I'm not sure travelling puppet shows even exist anymore. No matter, seeing this particular show was a life-changing moment. Not only because I got to go swimming afterwards, and I loved swimming, but also because I got to meet one of my favourite TV stars: Sweep.

After the puppet show concluded (no doubt with a huge glittery magic stunt performed by Sooty), the scores of children in rapturous attendance were asked to go up to the 'performance stage' to shake the 'hands' of the 'performers'. This was almost too much for me to bear!

'Move along, Sooty,' I shouted. 'Get out the way, Soo,' I screamed at the panda of the gang. I jumped to the front of the queue, and made a beeline straight for Sweep – the only super dog that mattered to me as a small boy. I think I got Sweep's autograph on this momentous occasion, but I might be misremembering this, as I'm not sure how a glove puppet could sign its name without spoiling the illusion of not being a hand inside a glove. Anyway, I remember chatting to Sweep for quite some time; his answers were always short and sweet – but then, that's Sweep for you.

Created by master puppeteer, and all-round nice man, Harry Corbett, *The Sooty Show* first aired in 1955. I started watching the programme in the 1980s – as did a lot of schoolchildren my age – when the show was in its third incarnation, and no longer on the BBC, but on ITV instead. I remember the interminable adverts, agonisingly waiting for the show to begin. Sweep, for those of you who do not know what I am going on about, is a grey glove puppet with long black ears and a red nose, who made a very annoying 'squeak' every time he 'spoke'. He had joined the Sooty Show in 1957 as Sooty's best friend. While Sooty made a fool of himself doing bad magic tricks, while often saying 'Izzy Whizzy, let's get busy!', Sweep would be found tucking into a never-ending string of sausages and generally flailing about with his legs in the air, the constant victim of Sooty and Soo's slapstick mayhem. While it is often assumed that Sweep was the stupid one of the gang, I always found there was a quiet dignity in the way he wore wellington boots, and Sooty didn't. 'He must be quite clever if he wears wellies,' I remember saying to my mum.

Sweep has three brothers (Swoop, Swipe and Swap), though I don't remember being that fond of them. For me, it was Sweep or nothing. I could even take or leave Sooty.

In 1975, Harry's son, Matthew, took over presenting the iconic show and, for me as a child of the eighties, he was the puppeteer that helped cement Sooty, Sweep and Soo in the hearts and minds of a new generation. Their daily misadventures used to have me, and no doubt them too, in stitches, and I hope they carry on for another fifty years!

Did You Know?

The phrase 'raining cats and dogs' originated in seventeenth-century England. During heavy rainstorms, many homeless animals would drown and float down the streets, giving the appearance that it had actually 'rained cats and dogs'.

SNOOPY

Snoopy is one of the world's most beloved super dogs. He found fame as the star of the comic strip, *Peanuts*, alongside TV shows and animated films that would make Snoopy one of the all-time greatest dog characters ever created.

On 4 October 1950, Snoopy first appeared in the comic strip *Peanuts*, a creation of the imaginative mind of comic artist Charles Schulz. Snoopy, at first, was a minor character, the loveable oddball pet, and comic foil, of 'depressing loser' Charlie Brown. However, Snoopy's popularity grew – as did that of *Peanuts* – and fans of the comic strip insisted that Schulz draw more of Snoopy into Charlie's storylines alongside Patty and Linus, Schulz's other great character creations. Pretty soon the long-eared beagle was the face of *Peanuts*, making Charlie Brown very jealous. He became an internationally recognised figure, a dog that all people could connect with, a dog that would bark instantly quotable lines that were distinctly human: 'Sit up, lie down, roll over, play dead? Everything's the same, day in, day out. I need – a change.' Well said, Snoopy. Hear! Hear!

Indeed, Snoopy's quirks, quotes and dog-philosophy became famous. He became known for lying flat on top of his doghouse, pondering life, the universe and what exactly Charlie Brown did at school all day; he would pretend he was a World War One airplane pilot or a Foreign Legionnaire; he would don thick black sunglasses and immediately become Joe Cool – his sanguine and laid-back alter ego; and he would hang out with his yellow bird-friend Woodstock, offering sage advice and wisdom.

Charles Schulz died in February 2000, just days after he retired Snoopy and the gang, announcing he was 'no longer able to maintain the schedule demanded by a daily comic strip. My family does not wish *Peanuts* to be continued by anyone else, therefore I am announcing my retirement.'

Schulz also said that 'drawing Snoopy and friends was the fulfillment of my childhood ambition'. Imagine drawing Snoopy all day for a living? Charles Schulz did indeed live the dream and, for fifty amazing years, he gave the world a character that mirrored and reflected how they felt, and how they *could* feel, and all through the eyes of a smart, quirky and loveable dog.

Though Schulz is sadly no longer with us, Snoopy's legacy lives on. Most notably in my loft, where there is a plethora of Snoopy and Woodstock cuddly toys, books and old comics that I am keeping for when my children are grown-up enough to appreciate them properly. The legacy of super dog Snoopy must be preserved.

 Happiness is a warm puppy.

CHARLES M. SCHULZ

SNOWY

He may be a fictional super dog, but in the minds of Hergé's readers' imaginations Snowy comes to life as one of the great classic crime-fighting super dogs who always gets his man!

As a child I whiled away many a sunny summer afternoon soaking in the exotic adventures of Tintin, a teenage Indiana Jones with a ginger quiff, and his wonder-dog, Snowy. The white-haired fox terrier was more than Tintin's loyal sidekick, constantly nipping at the heels of the young sleuth's nemesis, Red Rackham. He was a fully fleshed-out character, with actual speech bubbles above his head to show his internal monologue. He was as integral to the story as Tintin or Captain Haddock and was always at the centre of the action. Much of the time, it was Snowy's nose for trouble that kick-started the adventures!

Snowy and Tintin's first appearance, in the legendary comic books written by the Belgian cartoonist Hergé, occurred in 1929, which means that Snowy, in dog years, is around 600 years old – and still going strong!

Tintin and Snowy finally made it to the big screen in Steven Spielberg's amazing *The Adventures of Tintin: The Secret of the Unicorn*. Most praise for the film, though, ended up in Snowy's lap; Spielberg's hyper-real visualisation of the dog looked stunning in 3D – you could almost reach out and touch him. But, of course, for true fans of Snowy, like me, nothing compares to the original adventures in comic book form.

Did You Know?

The longest dog tail ever measured on record was 28.46 inches (72.29 cm). Wagged by Finnegan, an Irish wolfhound, from Calgary, Canada, on 15 August 2013.

ICONIC SUPER DOGS OF HISTORY

The history books we carried around in our backpacks at school are full of courageous men and women. But what about the super dogs of history, the truly special dogs whose names will live forever? Let's take a look at some of the most iconic...

THE DOG THAT ATE MY HOMEWORK

The first ever dog to eat homework was Henry Pennywhistle's dog. Though his name was never recorded, he was a super dog indeed!

Since homework was invented – which I imagine was a few centuries ago – kids have been trying their very best not to do it. There have been hundreds, thousands, possibly even millions of excuses deployed from the mouths of children to worm, wriggle and wangle their way out of doing schoolwork at home. History's best excuse of them all – and the most imaginative – has to be: THE DOG ATE MY HOMEWORK.

I don't recall ever using it myself – I was too much of a goodie-two-shoes – but I know kids who did and it always sounded hilarious, even if the repercussions weren't. Anyway, the first recorded utterance of this brilliant, dog-faced lie took place – according to education historian Christopher Simpson – on 12 January 1835, spoken by a wisecracking student by the name of Henry Pennywhistle. But imagine if it wasn't a made-up excuse at all – *what if the dog did actually eat Pennywhistle's homework*? What if he was telling the truth? It would mean that poor old Pennywhistle has gone down in history as a liar and a cheat, when actually it was all his dog's fault after all!

If that is the case, then Pennywhistle's dog was not only a very hungry doggy, but also a very naughty one. Nonetheless, the dog and its appetite for learning (as well as eating said learning), has transcended generations of schoolboys and schoolgirls and he should, therefore, be celebrated as a mighty fine super dog.*

Did You Know?

Thirty-six per cent of dog owners have bought clothing for their dogs.

---

* With the obvious use of digital technology in many of today's classrooms (homework is now sent via email rather than handed in, I imagine), the phrase 'The dog ate my homework' will surely die with this current generation, leaving schoolchildren of the future to become even more inventive – 'Miss, the dog ate my laptop!'

GREYFRIARS BOBBY

Greyfriars Bobby, a loveable Skye terrier, is Scotland's most famous dog. His heartbreaking loyalty is known the world over and was immortalised in the Disney movie called, imaginatively, *Greyfriars Bobby*.

Before he was known as Greyfriars Bobby, Greyfriars Bobby was actually just a wee doggy called Bobby (this sentence sounds funniest in a broad Scottish accent). From a pup, Bobby had 'belonged' to John Gray, a nightwatchman for the Edinburgh city police.

He grew up to be a feisty, faithful terrier who never left his owner's side. When Gray died, in 1858, he was buried at the Greyfriars Kirkyard, the graveyard surrounding Greyfriars Kirk in Edinburgh. Bobby – so the story goes – sat down on his master's grave, but not just for a few days. Not even for a few months. But for fourteen years.

Bobby never left his master's side, and survived on the scraps of food left for him by passers-by who started to take notice of mournful Bobby's graveside companionship. Bobby became a bit of a local celebrity, with many people checking in on him to make sure he was OK.

In 1872, Bobby died, still firmly perched on his master's grave. In honour of his loyalty, Bobby was buried just inside the gate of Greyfriars Kirkyard – animals, no matter how loyal, were usually forbidden to be buried inside the graveyard. He remains at rest only a stone's throw from his master.

While there are many variations of such stories about dog loyalty, there is something about this particular dog tale that makes me happy. While I doubt my own dog would mourn me for that long, it always raises a smile on my face to remember that a dog often makes a very real connection with its human counterpart, a bond sometimes strong enough to defy the laws of nature, a bond that occasionally not even death can break.

Did You Know?

Thirty-eight per cent of dog owners own up to having a picture of their dog in their wallet.

PERITAS

Let us turn back in time to around 300 BC, the age of Alexander the Great and his loyal and trusty dog companion, Peritas...

You've probably almost forgotten learning about him during history lessons at school, but Alexander the Great was a conqueror who created one of the largest empires the world has ever known, one that stretched from modern-day Greece to Pakistan, and who was never defeated in battle. But all of that was thanks to Peritas, his trusty companion, who never left his side.

As loyal dogs go, Peritas sets the standard for all other super dogs to aspire to. Little is known of this fierce creature – maybe he was a Molosser, possibly a pit bull, but definitely not a chihuahua. What is known is that this furry ally accompanied Alexander on his decade-long war tour, his empire-expansion programme, throughout Asia, the Middle East and North Africa, while Alexander was slashing and burning his way through the known world.

Alexander the Great ended up a renowned military leader, with many of his tactics still discussed at military academies throughout the world. But Peritas was pretty tasty in a fight, too. According to the legends that surround Alexander, Peritas fought off and slew a lion and an elephant – during the same fight! That's pretty super, but it was Peritas's final honourable and lifesaving act that picks up this particular dog and throws it high into the upper echelons of super-dog superiority.

During an intense and lengthy battle in Egypt, Peritas's loyal master was struck and pinned down by a javelin; he was unable to free himself. Seeing his master fall, and in mortal peril from an incoming enemy horde, Peritas jumped onto Alexander's approaching foes, giving him just enough time to be pulled away by his soldiers.

Peritas, according to the legend, died in the same battle, himself being pierced by a javelin in the chest. The only comfort Peritas had in his last moments was that he died in Alexander's lap. In commemoration, and celebration, of his doggy pal who saved his life, Alexander the Great – one of history's most feared conquerors – is said to have built a city in his honour.

Did You Know?

Forty-one per cent of dog owners admit to letting their dogs sleep in their bed.

LADY ET AL.

Lady, a very small Pomeranian puppy, survived the sinking of the very large and 'unsinkable' *Titanic*. But, thankfully, Lady wasn't alone. Two other dogs made it safely back to shore, too. Let's take a look...

Out of the twelve dogs – all belonging to super-wealthy first-class passengers, it should be noted – that boarded the RMS *Titanic* on that fateful voyage on 14 April 1912, only three young pups survived. One of these dogs, a Pomeranian named Lady, became one of history's luckiest survivors. Owned by Margaret Hays, she was a pet with a difference. Born into wealth and society, the appropriately named Lady was a first-class passenger on the ill-fated maiden voyage of this first of a new class of luxury superliners constructed by the prestigious White Star Line.

It was en route to New York City that the 'unsinkable' ship hit an iceberg in the early hours of 14 April, around 400 miles off the coast of Newfoundland (ironically, a breed of dog that would have been very handy to save lives in this disaster). As was to be expected, immediately after the liner starting filling up with vast volumes of ocean water, many of the lifeboats on board started becoming awfully popular, and incredibly crammed.

In a moment of arrogance and improper disregard for the health and safety of their passengers, the White Star Line had not provided the *Titanic* with enough lifeboats to save all of the 3,000 occupants, and many of the lifeboats that were deployed, it transpired afterwards, had sailed away from the doomed liner half-empty.

Lady was lucky enough to board one of the lifeboats, her owner having smuggled her tiny puppy in a blanket. The lifeboat crew allowed Mrs Hays to board, assuming Lady to be an infant baby swaddled in clothes. Little did they know it was a small dog.

Meanwhile, as chaos reigned on board the ship, a Pekinese by the name of Sun-Yat Sen had also been concealed aboard a lifeboat. The third dog to survive was another Pomeranian, owned by the Rothschilds.

Out of the wreckage of the *Titanic* survived a story that made it back to land – but this story is not of a super dog, but of a super dog owner. A first-class passenger by the name of Ann Elizabeth Isham was said to have been on board a lifeboat ready to sail away from the sinking ship, *but had got out*, when she was told that she was unable to bring her dog, a Great Dane, on board with her. He was just too big, the lifeboat crew argued, and took up valuable space. In the days that followed, many rescue ships were sent to the site of the vessel's watery grave to recover any survivors, as well as the floating dead. From on board one of these rescue ships, a crew member reported seeing the strange, unforgettable sight of a woman's body floating in the ocean. It was Mrs Isham, deceased, but afloat on flotsam and jetsam and apparently holding on to the body of her beloved dog. She may not have been able to save his life, but then, she had decided that she could not continue hers without him.*

---

* This entry is a tribute to the nine other dogs on board the *Titanic* that, sadly, did not survive the disaster, including a fox terrier named Dog, an Airedale named Kitty, and Gamin de Pycombe, a French bulldog. The names of the other dogs that were on board are not known.

Did You Know?

The loudest bark by a dog was recorded at 108 decibels, produced by white German shepherd, Daz, in Finsbury Park, London, 15 June 2009.

PAL (AKA LASSIE)

Pal was, without a doubt, a gorgeous dog. You know her by the stage name Lassie, the famous collie standing proudly on top of the hill, but how much do you really know about Pal? Was she even a girl?

An intelligent and fearless dog that made the perilous journey home from Scotland to Yorkshire to be reunited with her young master, Lassie was the creation of British writer Eric Knight, who owned a collie called Toots while living in California. His book *Lassie Come Home* was made into a successful Hollywood movie, starring Roddy McDowall as Lassie's young best friend.

More movies set in England and Scotland followed, but Pal and many of her offspring in fact went on to become stars of American TV. Radio shows, novels and comic books followed, as Lassie became the face of countless products from dog food to board games. So successful were the all-American family TV series over a twenty-year period that Lassie from Yorkshire ended up a lasting icon of the American Dream.

But Pal wasn't in fact the first choice of collie to play Lassie for the original feature film. During pre-production of *Lassie Come Home* – the event that kick-started an entire nation's love affair with Lassie in the USA – MGM conducted a nationwide search to find a female collie star that had the on-screen gravitas to play the heroic dog. They found one, whose name has since been consigned to history's bins, and assigned the now legendary Hollywood dog trainer Frank Weatherwax to handle her.

During one of the film's earliest action sequences, when the original leading lady refused to jump into a swollen river, Weatherwax offered the film director his own male collie, Pal, as a substitute. Straight away, under his owner's command, Pal swam across the dangerous river and then crawled onto the riverbank as if exhausted by the drama of it all. Exactly what the director required for the scene. This dramatic bit of acting by Pal made Louis B. Mayer – MGM's notorious studio head and the film's producer – excitedly proclaim, 'That dog may have jumped in the water as Pal, but he came out as Lassie.' From that day on, Pal *was* Lassie and the rest is history. The glamorous Lassie has been played by male dogs ever since.

Did You Know?

The record for a dog removing banknotes from a wallet in one minute is six. Accomplished by Ben, a Japanese spaniel, on 2 June 2012.

DIAMOND

Diamond. One of history's most elusive hounds that reportedly nearly killed Sir Isaac Newton and almost ruined the publication of one of the most important scientific breakthroughs ever...

Sir Isaac Newton doesn't need any introduction – you know who he is and what he did*. But you may have never heard of Diamond, or even that Newton owned a dog. Diamond's owner was one of the most celebrated scientists the world has known, but because so little is known of Newton's private life, the only evidence we have of Diamond is through letters and correspondence that Newton sent, a few casual references here and there. In order to learn more about the dog, we must first learn a little bit more about the man...

Science historians have various notes and letters that suggest Newton had few friends; he was unable to successfully engage with the opposite sex and had very few close personal relationships throughout his long life. Newton's relationship with his mother was considered 'complex' (historians agree that she abandoned him) and he never had children. The only evidence that Newton cared for or was compassionate about

---

* Quick refresher course: Newton discovered the law of gravity, invented modern physics with his Three Laws of Motion, and devised calculus. He is often referred to as the single most important scientist the world has ever known.

anything other than his earth-shattering scientific endeavours was his relationship with his dog. Newton loved his dog. Not as much as science, clearly, but still he loved her.

Diamond was a creamy-white female Pomeranian, and a feisty one at that. The scant details we have of her, through Newton's letters to his peers, demonstrate that she was protective, a good watch dog, and prone to causing trouble.

In one letter, Newton described an event that was responsible for 'why his publication on the treatise that contained his law of gravity would be delayed'. Newton, so the story goes, was putting the finishing revisions to a manuscript he was working on, complete with important calculations and equations. It was getting dark so Newton decided to light a few candles. Diamond was sleeping in a corner of the room dreaming her doggy dreams, when Newton heard a knock at the front door. The scientist briefly left the room, with the dog, the candles and the manuscript still in it. Suffice to say, when Newton came back into the room a few minutes later, the dog was awake, the manuscript was on fire and the room was about to become engulfed in flames.

Seemingly, the noise of unfamiliar voices at the front door had awoken Diamond, who, in an excited frenzy of barking and movement to protect her owner, and fresh from slumber, had knocked over the candles on the table onto her master's manuscript, setting the untidy notes ablaze. When Newton returned to the room he was aghast at the scene that was unfolding. Bad-dog Diamond had set back Newton's publication date, and therefore one of the most important scientific developments of the world, by months! Diamond was in the doghouse, and Newton was back at the drawing board.

While we know very little about Diamond, and indeed Newton, I like to think that this story is true. I also like to think that it is perhaps because of Diamond that Newton was able to first dream up his calculations. Who knows, in the quiet moments in the middle of the night, when Newton was scratching his chin, stuck on an idea, and contemplating the complex and confusing law of gravity, maybe it was a small stroke of Diamond's belly or head that could have provided sufficient clarity of thought, that might have de-stressed and unwound a famously clogged mind. Diamond could have been the pivotal stress relief that allowed Newton to think BIG. And that is why, for me, Diamond is (probably) a super dog!

Did You Know?

Nine per cent of dog owners admit that their dogs have Facebook pages... that they (the owners) set up!

TERRY

Toto, a male cairn terrier, was Dorothy Gale's loyal companion on her adventures in Oz. But Toto wasn't actually Toto at all, to paraphrase Dorothy. No, Toto was in fact Terry. And he was not a boy, but a girl. Let's meet her.

Born in 1933, Terry is remembered as one of the world's most famous on-screen sidekicks. She appeared, of course, in the 1939 classic *The Wizard of Oz*, but what you may have not known is that Terry also performed in another fifteen movies, including the famous Shirley Temple vehicle *Bright Eyes*, as the loveable Rags.

The Wizard of Oz creator, L. Frank Baum, originally described Toto, in the children's classic tale published in 1900, as 'a little black dog with long silky hair and small black eyes that twinkled merrily on either side of his funny, wee nose'. And, thanks to the glorious use of the Technicolor employed ever so cleverly in the film adaptation, we got to see Toto just as the author detailed, its bright black coat providing a balanced contrast to the strong beams of colour hailing from Dorothy's red ruby slippers and the almost too bright, in-your-face glare of the yellow brick road.

Interestingly, during the making of the film, Terry was paid a salary of $125 a week, far more than several of the human actors. The dwarfs, for example, who played the beloved

Munchkins, reportedly only received $50 a week. Now, I'm all for dog-equality, even dog-superiority, but paying human actors less than the dog on a movie set is highly embarrassing for all involved. Except the dog.

 A dog desires affection more than its dinner. Well – almost.

CHARLOTTE GRAY

HOBO

The Littlest Hobo, or simply 'Hobo' to those people he helped, was perhaps the most famous dog in the world in the 1980s – a big achievement considering dogs on TV were all the rage back then.

The Littlest Hobo was more than just a show with a great theme tune. It was also a show with a fantastically simple but brilliant concept: dog goes from town to town saving people.

That's it.

And, for six seasons over six years, that's all that happened. Hobo would turn up out of the blue and just start helping humans. Nobody asked questions about who the dog was or whether it belonged to anyone, they were just thankful for the help. The show played on the concept of 'the kindness of strangers' almost too much. Hobo's origin and backstory were never revealed, giving very little emotional understanding of who the black-and-white German shepherd was or why he was compelled to be so kind to strangers for nothing in return.

Here are some very genuine descriptions of some of Hobo's greatest weekly adventures and achievements – I've chosen a handful of the most ludicrous:

🐾 Hobo comes to the rescue of a downed balloonist.

🐾 Hobo helps find a hijacked truckload of diamonds.

- Hobo befriends a young basketball player who is having problems being accepted by his teammates.

- Hobo turns health inspector when botulism is discovered at a campground.

- Hobo foils sabotage at a courier service.

- Hobo befriends a lonely clown (my favourite).

- Hobo happens upon a real crime on a movie set.

- Hobo helps spur romance between a widow and a bachelor.

- Hobo witnesses a wilderness plane crash and aids the victims.

- Hobo aids elderly people fleeing a retirement home (another favourite).

There are dozens more high-quality episodes just like these, with some utterly compelling storylines that in this cynical modern age just couldn't happen. However, wouldn't it be great if TV executives gave *The Littlest Hobo* a reboot for the twenty-first century? Imagine the sorts of adventures Hobo could get up to this time around:

- Hobo helps an old lady set up her Facebook profile.

- Hobo helps a teenager pass her driving test at the first attempt.

- Hobo appears as a talent-show winner's manager and helps them negotiate a long-term six-album deal with Simon Cowell's record label.

Did You Know?

Since the Battersea Dogs and Cats Home opened in 1860, they've taken in over three million dogs and cats.

FIDO

Abraham Lincoln is one of America's most famous presidents. He also had a very famous dog – a dog whose name would inspire the naming of dogs forever more. You know his name. Fido...

Lincoln was America's sixteenth president, and one of the greatest. Fido, a yellow Labrador, born circa 1855, was his faithful dog. In fact, 'fido' in Latin means 'I am faithful'. Lincoln was a huge fan of Latin, and could speak it well; possibly the only US president who could lay claim to that honour.

Lincoln loved pets and was a lifelong dog lover. He believed that animals provide a psychological and therapeutic value to humans. His relationship with dogs was once observed by his law partner, William Herndon, 'If exhausted from severe and long-continued thought, Lincoln had to touch the earth again to renew his strength. When this weariness set in he would stop thought, and get down with a little dog to recover.' Aw!

However, out of the many pets the Lincoln family owned – including rabbits, horses, turkeys and even two goats called Nanny and Nanko – one dog was favoured above all others: Fido. He was top dog in the Lincoln household and, even before Lincoln was elected president, Fido would follow his bearded friend around his hometown of Springfield, Illinois, USA on errands. It was often noted that Lincoln had a soft spot for the dog, forever feeding him scraps from the dining room table and letting him smush in dirt and mud around the house.

It reportedly drove Lincoln's wife, Mary Todd, around the bend, and she assured him that once they were in the White House they would not want an unruly dog running around, wagging its tail and knocking over priceless American artifacts.

So it was with great regret that, when Lincoln was elected president of the United States in 1861, poor Fido had to be left at home with a foster family in Springfield. Lincoln, it is said, wrote detailed instructions on how every dog-whim of Fido's had to be indulged by his new family. Fido was to be treated like a president, just as his master had treated him.

Due to a paucity of photographic evidence and nineteenth-century media stories, Fido's existence remained relatively unknown until newspapers in the early twentieth century started publishing articles about, and photographs of, Lincoln's faithful Fido – the dog that inspired such loyalty in one of the USA's most pioneering presidents.

As news spread of Fido's loyalty and companionship to the great Lincoln, the name Fido became more and more popular in the US, eventually becoming the go-to dog name for many decades, hitting a peak in the 1960s.

Sadly, Lincoln never made it back to his hometown to see his furry chum. The president's assassin, John Wilkes Booth, saw to that. But as I write this, I like to think that, with Lincoln and Fido both dying in 1865 (reports have suggested that Fido was stabbed to death by a drunk man that year), they are together now, laughing about the good ol' days back in Springfield, Illinois.

 I care not for a man's religion whose dog and cat are not the better for it.

ABRAHAM LINCOLN

CAP

Florence Nightingale is history's celebrated healer of the sick. But, as this heartwarming story will show, Florence's dream of changing the world could actually have been inspired by events involving some very naughty teenage boys and a sheepdog called Cap...

Celebrated in dog-eared history books as the founder of modern nursing, and dubbed the 'Lady of the Lamp' on account of her night-time rounds while treating the wounded soldiers of the Crimean War, Nightingale dedicated her entire life to the care of the sick and the war-wounded. By the end of the Crimean War in 1854, she was a living legend, remembered by the soldiers she had cared for and comforted in their time of need. She then established a nursing school at St Thomas' Hospital, London, and would later become the first woman to be given the British Order of Merit. But all of these achievements may have not been possible without a simple encounter with a dog in pain. A sheepdog named Cap.

Put on your time-travelling hats, and let us go back in history to a sunny afternoon in Matlock, Derbyshire. The year is 1837. On this day, local village teenagers, boys, of course, decided it was a good idea to start throwing stones at Cap, a sheepdog who belonged to a local shepherd called Roger. Cap didn't deserve this; he was simply sleeping in a doorway. He was hit on his leg, and was so badly injured that he was unable to stand or run away from the onslaught of stones.

After the boys had fled, leaving Cap badly bleeding and bruised, Roger found his dog and was distraught. This shepherd could not go to work without a working sheepdog, and could not afford to keep a dog that couldn't work. And so it was with a heavy heart that Roger left Cap to go and find a piece of rope with which he would hang his beloved dog.

It was while Roger was finding this rope that a seventeen-year-old girl, Florence, happened to wander by. Starting a conversation with the obviously upset shepherd, she asked what was wrong. Roger began to tell her about Cap's injuries and the teenager was so distressed by the events of the morning that she reportedly decided that she ought to at least take a look at Cap and see if there was anything she could do to help. She visited Roger's farm and took a detailed look at Cap's injuries to examine the damage done. She assessed that, while Cap's leg was indeed badly injured, it was not broken. Roger did not need to put down his faithful dog – all Cap needed was some TLC and time for the wounds to heal.

She spent time bandaging Cap's leg and stayed by his side that evening to cover the wounds and prevent infection. A few days later, she returned to check on Cap and his progress. He was still limping, but it was immediately clear to her that her first patient had survived and would make a full recovery.

But this is not the end of the story. What happened next changed Florence's life forever...

On the evening of 7 February 1837, Florence Nightingale had a dream. A vision, perhaps. This dream caused her to believe that she had heard the voice of God, that the Almighty had spoken directly to her... and that he had a plan for her: to devote her life to healing the sick and caring for the dying.

Healing Cap, having faith in his recovery, and attending to his near-fatal wounds, had awoken a deep spiritual feeling within Nightingale – it had given her not just a purpose, but also a mission. She reportedly believed that the incident of Cap's malicious stoning was a sign from God to tell her that she should devote her life to protecting others. As dreams go, it was a pretty good one. And, as the saying goes, the rest is history.

So, next time you hear about the miracles of Florence Nightingale, remember that all of her good work, and the countless lives she saved, could have been inspired by the actions of some very naughty boys who refused to let a sleeping dog lie and a lucky dog called Cap that she brought back to life.

Did You Know?

Dog-walking boosts the chances of social encounters, with 74 per cent of dog owners feeling that their pet allows them to socialise more.

BLONDI

A controversial entry, but a super dog nonetheless – if only because of the owner this dog had to put up with. But she could also climb ladders. Ladies and gentlemen, may I introduce you to Blondi, Adolf Hitler's beloved pet dog...

Adolf Hitler and his Nazi party need no introduction. Everything that probably needs to be written about Hitler has already been written. But Blondi, Hitler's favourite German shepherd (did you know Hitler loved dogs?) definitely deserves an introduction – and to be celebrated and praised as a super dog.

Poor Blondi not only died in the most tragic and disgusting circumstances, but her owner committed so many atrocities during his life that no dog would want to belong to the man in the first place.

Not a lot of people know this but Adolf, in German, means 'noble wolf'; so it's hardly surprising to learn of Hitler's affinity with dogs. In 1941 Blondi was given as a present to Hitler by his private secretary and right-hand man, and wildly inhumane human being, Martin Bormann. According to diaries and letters written by Hitler between 1941 and 1945, he became very fond of his pet dog; everywhere he went, she went, forever staying by his side and even sleeping in his bedroom. Photos taken of Hitler in the 1940s illustrate that Blondi was a constant companion of the dictator, and a very loyal companion right up to the end, too loyal, in fact, but then that is to be expected from the German shepherd breed. It was reported, however, that Hitler's love affair with Blondi was not shared by Eva Braun, Hitler's mistress, then wife (they got married the day before they both died after realising that their lives would soon be taken from them).

On 29 April 1945, Hitler began hearing rumours of the sudden execution of his staunch ally, Italy's fascist leader Benito Mussolini. Hitler knew by then that the war was lost – the Soviet army had beaten the German army on the Eastern Front and were soon to be marching into Berlin. Hitler's main concern now was not allowing himself or Braun to be captured.

That afternoon, Hitler received a batch of cyanide capsules he had ordered from Bormann, ready to be taken in the inevitable event of things turning bad. To verify the cyanide potency and dosage within the capsules (Hitler was adamant the dose must be lethal), Hitler ordered his doctor to test them on Blondi. Hitler feared that if the cyanide capsules did not kill himself and Eva, they would inevitably be arrested. As a result of Hitler's suicidal perfectionism, Blondi was force-fed a fatal dose of cyanide and died instantly, leaving Hitler immediately inconsolable.

The next day, on 30 April 1945, as Soviet troops completely surrounded Berlin, Braun used a cyanide capsule to commit suicide and Hitler shot himself in the head; their bodies were then dragged upstairs and burnt. According to eyewitness accounts, Hitler's dog-handler, Fritz Tornow, had been ordered to take Blondi's pups outside the bunker and shoot them in the garden within minutes of receiving the news that Hitler and Braun were dead. This was, reportedly, one of Hitler's last commands as Führer before shooting himself.

 My little dog – a heartbeat at my feet.

EDITH WHARTON

Rufus

Britain's greatest prime minister, decisive wartime leader and unstoppable quote-machine, Winston Churchill, is often commonly associated with the bulldog. However, it was actually a miniature poodle named Rufus that should forever remind us of Sir Winston...

Churchill, regularly voted Number One Briton of all time, had the jowls of a bulldog. He looked like a bulldog. He used to famously blame his distinctly squidgy face and fifty chins on the sweet iced frosting on top of cupcakes, which – if rumour is to be believed – was also invented by the great man himself.

Churchill often acted, politically, like a bulldog. He spoke as I imagine a bulldog would speak; all gruff and deep. His nickname was the 'British Bulldog'. Everything we believe we know about Churchill's canine leanings suggests that he was more closely tied to the bulldog breed than any other – physically, mentally and metaphorically. But that is a long way from the real truth.

Churchill loved poodles. Yes, poodles. And not man-sized ones, either. Miniature poodles. Very small ginger poodles. And one poodle in particular had a special place in his heart. A poodle named Rufus. Churchill loved the dog so much that after Rufus was run over and killed while Churchill was attending a Conservative Party Conference in Brighton in

October 1947, he was so distraught that he was given another miniature poodle by his friend Walter Graebner, the editor of the prestigious *Life* magazine. When Churchill introduced this new Rufus at social functions he would say, 'His name is Rufus II – but the II is silent.' How cute!

Both Rufuses were treated like members of his family and they always ate in the dining room with the rest of the Churchill clan. A cloth was laid on the floor for them on the Persian carpet beside the head of the household (Churchill), and no one could start eating until the butler had served their meal.

One classic Churchill anecdote regarding Rufus (MK II) refers to one evening the family, including Winston's wife Clementine and their five grown-up children, spent watching the film *Oliver Twist* while in residence at Chequers, the prime minister's holiday home. Rufus, as usual, was sitting on his master's lap, always the best seat in the house for any dog, being stroked as the film's glorious plot unfolded in front of them. At the point in the movie when the character Bill Sikes was about to drown his dog to divert the police from his track, Churchill covered Rufus's eyes with his hand and leant down and whispered in his ear, 'Don't look now, dear. I'll tell you about it afterwards.' Isn't it amazing to think that even historic world leaders can love their dogs as much as the rest of us?*

 Our dog chases people on a bike. We've had to take it off him.

WINSTON CHURCHILL

---

* Churchill once wrote a poem for his daughter's sick pug dog. The poem went: 'Pet him and kiss him and give him a hug, run and fetch him a suitable drug, wrap him up all tenderly in a rug, that is the way to cure Puggy-wug.'

LAIKA

The mongrel Laika – part husky, part terrier – is an international dog-hero. A former Moscow stray, this champion super dog became the first living creature to orbit the earth!

On 3 November 1957, the USSR space agency launched the second of its historic Sputnik satellites. These artificial satellites were momentous achievements in the developing space race – and Cold War stand-off – between the Soviet Union and the USA, and were the first indicators that led many observers to believe that, ultimately, the USSR would be the first nation to put a man on the moon. Ahead of the Apollo missions, Neil Armstrong and those big ol' giant leaps for mankind, Laika's one-way trip to space was a giant leap forward for 'dog kind'. And it was a mission that stunned the entire world.

A month previous to Laika's launch, the Soviets had launched Sputnik 1, another metal satellite, but much lighter than Sputnik 2 and with no occupants on board. Sputnik 1's launch was a resounding success and the mission has been praised as the first artificial satellite in space. The satellite, complete with its four radio antennae, was able to provide vital data and information for space scientists back down on earth. But, more importantly than that, Sputnik 1's launch was the first political chess piece to be moved in what was to become a long-running space race with the US.

All of a sudden, space became the new playground, and the USA and the USSR rushed to prove who had the biggest toys. However, no one outside of the USSR – including NASA and the US government – was expecting there to be a passenger on board Sputnik 1's follow-up mission.

The Soviets' announcement of a space voyager sent shockwaves around the world, and Laika's position as the first dog to fly sent the international agencies and communities into a frenzy. Indeed, when the Soviets admitted, pre-flight, that Laika would die on Sputnik 2 and never return safely to earth, many observers (probably dog lovers) were outraged. The hastily organised flight meant that Soviet command simply could not wait to work out a re-entry strategy for the satellite. Nobody, it seemed, in the USSR at least, was too bothered that a dog was on a kamikaze mission, that they were sending a dog to its certain death.

Russian for 'barker', the name Laika has gone down in the history books as a first-of-a-kind triumphant moment in mankind's desire to conquer space – Laika was not only the first living creature to leave the earth's atmosphere, she was also the first living creature to orbit the earth.

While on board Sputnik 2, effectively a 250 lb (113 kilo) metal sphere constantly sending flight data and scientific information back to earth, Laika was chained down to prevent her from moving, while connected to lots of instrumentation which monitored various elements of her health. The Soviet officials responsible for the mission (and for Laika's well-being) announced that she would be euthanised prior to the satellite's oxygen depletion on the sixth day of orbit.

Until 2002, many scientists believed – having been reported by Soviet officials as fact – that Laika had survived the launch and died painlessly almost a week after Sputnik's blast-off. Sadly, recent investigations into Laika's lauded flight show that the dog's fate did not go to plan. In fact, now Russian investigators can say with authority that while Laika did indeed heroically survive the bumpy launch and dangerous flight five miles into space (where she became the first creature to encounter weightlessness), the monitors connected all over her body indicated that after five to seven hours into the flight no life signs were being received. By the fourth orbit of earth – and not the fourth day as reported by Soviet space officials – it was apparent that Laika had died from overheating, panic and stress. The poor thing.

While the more recent investigation dug up a lot of unpleasant facts about Laika's last few hours alive, I like to think that in her last few moments Laika managed to look out the window and get a good view of the heavens above and below, and know that her place as a true super dog was assured forever. As well as providing vital information that a living creature could tolerate treacherous space conditions, such as weightlessness and being strapped to a huge fiery rocket, Laika's flight and initial survival out of earth's atmosphere inspired humans to follow in her dog steps.

Sputnik 2, with Laika's body inside, circled the earth 2,570 times before burning up on re-entry to the earth's atmosphere on 4 April 1958 – five months after Laika's historic launch. In 2008, Russian officials erected a small monument to Laika, near the military research facility where she was trained.

Did You Know?

The record for jump-rope skips completed by a dog in one minute is seventy-five. This feat was achieved by Sweet Pea, an Australian shepherd/Border collie cross, in New York on 8 August 2007.

BELKA AND STRELKA

It's time to read about the dangerous adventures of two stray dogs called Belka and Strelka – space dogs extraordinaire. Of course, they had no choice in the matter, but, don't worry, this story has a happy ending...

While Laika was the first super dog to orbit the earth, it would be remiss of me not to also mention the brave, bold and significant second and third super dogs who not only flew in space and successfully orbited the planet, but also *safely* returned home to earth. These super dogs may have only followed in another dog's paw-steps, but their safe return home was a key turning point in history for two reasons:

- From this point on, dogs that were sent into space no longer faced certain death. (Thirteen dogs in total were sent into space.)

- It made the Americans hurry up with their space programme, which in turn prompted the Soviets to send cosmonaut Yuri Gagarin up ahead of schedule. Once the first human was sent into space, dogs no longer needed to be the guinea pigs.

So who were these adventurous little dogs? Belka and Strelka were two Russian mixed breeds, who went into space aboard the Soviets' Sputnik 5 satellite and became the first animals to survive a space journey.

In the 1960s, scientists believed that dogs were the best animals for this type of mission because dogs were well suited to 'long periods of inactivity'. Due to the 'success' of Laika's Sputnik 2 mission, Belka and Strelka were chosen as the perfect dogs as they too were strays who performed well in 'training' (i.e. kept in small boxes for up to twenty days at a time). And because they were strays, scientists believed that they were capable of coping with the stresses of space flight better than your average pet pooch.

While it could be argued that the scientists did all the hard work and the two dogs just sat strapped in their chairs, desperate to stick their heads out the window to feel the wind, the dogs were much more important than that: they proved that it was possible to send *something living* into space and get it back *still living*. Belka and Strelka were proof – just by sitting in Sputnik 5 – that the technology the scientists had built on earth could take the strain of lift-off, space travel and landing. Up until this time, they'd only achieved two out of three.

So, on 19 August 1960, Belka and Strelka were rocketed to their fate – no doubt they were very confused and bewildered about *where* they were going, but nonetheless very happy to be going on a trip. When they landed they were not only alive, they were also the first surviving cosmonauts (dogmonauts?).

Belka and Strelka were on board Sputnik 5 for twenty-five hours, made seventeen trips around the planet and arrived home in time for lunch and treats the next day. But they were no longer just unloved scrappy strays. Now they were heroes.

 A dog has one aim in life... to bestow his heart.

J. R. ACKERLEY

PAVLOV'S DOGS

In honour of Pavlov's sixty dogs that took part in the Russian physiologist's groundbreaking, and mouth-watering, experiments...

Ivan Pavlov began experimenting with dogs, not because he didn't like them, but because he liked their company so much he decided to have a bit of fun with them. At least, that's what I like to think.

Like so many of mankind's great scientific and technological advances, classical conditioning, or Pavlovian conditioning as it is also known, was discovered accidentally after Pavlov began to notice some very strange, and also some very typical, behaviour in his dogs.

While many of Pavlov's peers, like Sigmund Freud, were looking inward in their attempts to work out the complex ids, egos and superegos of the constructed human psychology, he was having way too much fun with dogs to care about all that Freudian nonsense. Instead, he was looking at salivation in dogs, and their responses to being fed (or not).

He noticed that his dogs would begin to salivate whenever he entered the room, even when he was not bringing them any tasty treats or biscuits of the dog variety. At first, he considered this something of a nuisance – when you have lots of dogs salivating at once it can get very messy, not to mention slippery. Who wants to spend their time cleaning up that much dog slobber? But after a while, Pavlov started to take note. Literally.

In 1902, he started with the simple concept that there are some things that a dog does not need to learn. For example, dogs don't learn to salivate whenever they see food, because this reflex is 'hard-wired', just like blinking is hard-wired into us. Pavlov called this type of 'hard-wiring' an 'unconditioned response'. With dogs, he demonstrated the existence of the unconditioned response by presenting them with a bowl of food and measuring their salivary secretions (by placing a device on the side of the dog's head that captured the dripping saliva in a tube that had been inserted in the dog's muzzle).

However, when Pavlov discovered that dogs could learn to associate an object or event (e.g. the ringing of a bell) with food, and that the object or event alone would subsequently trigger the same slippery response as the food itself, he believed that he had made a unique scientific discovery, one that he spent the rest of his career devoted to. He won the Nobel Prize in Physiology and Medicine in 1904, so all that dog slobber and dog hair on his clothes wasn't for nothing.

Once he had reached the conclusion that the dogs in his lab had learned to associate food with the ringing of a bell, he deduced that this must have been *learned*, because the dogs at first did not do that, and then they did, so their behaviour *must have changed*. 'Yes,' he thought, '*dogs can learn.*'

While this experiment may sound like teaching old dogs new tricks, at the time it was a major discovery into their behaviour, and it has gone on to influence and strengthen mankind's relationship with the animal ever since. I like to think that it was Pavlov's close work with his dogs that showed us a) how clever they can be and b) how important dog slobber really is.

 Scratch a dog and you'll find a permanent job.

FRANKLIN P. JONES

CAESAR

Let us bow our heads in silent respect for Caesar, Edward VII's beloved fox terrier, the super dog who famously walked in front of kings and emperors at his master's funeral procession and captured the hearts of a nation.

There is an image of Caesar that will make you want to cry. I found it on Google when researching Edward VII. I had heard about him in one of the daily dog chats I have with various friends and couldn't wait to read up about him and, in particular, find this one particular photograph.

Edward VII, Queen Elizabeth's great-grandfather and the eldest son of Queen Victoria, ruled as King of the United Kingdom for nine years until his death in 1910, at the age of sixty-eight. At his funeral on 20 May 1910, hundreds of thousands of people – truly huge crowds – lined the streets to pay their respects and watch as Edward's funeral cortege rolled slowly through the streets of central London. This funeral procession was like no other that had been before. Following behind Edward's coffin were scores of international dignitaries, many on horseback, including princes, presidents, political leaders and emperors, who had travelled great distances to pay their own final respects.

But in front of all these VIPs was one member of the royal family who perhaps would mourn and miss Edward more than anybody: Caesar, his beloved fox terrier. A dog with a name as imperial as his position. To the people who lined the streets, the sight of Caesar trotting beside Edward's coffin, I imagine, was a sight they would never forget. A dead king and his mournful dog, side by side until the very end.

Within four years of Edward's death, Britain – and the whole of Europe – slid into a world war in which Britain's grip on world power would loosen forever. Edward had been referred to as 'the peacemaker' for his ideals and his attempts to bring together the countries of Europe, but it would all be in vain.

But that image, that unforgettable black and white photograph of Caesar walking alongside his king, perhaps signified and symbolised Britain at its very best. For me, Caesar and Edward's connection that day represented a golden, happy moment in history; a uniting of a dog and his master, and also a vision of a country connecting with a dog and understanding the loss and bereavement they shared.

 You'll never reach your destination if you stop to throw stones at every dog that barks.

WINSTON CHURCHILL

Rin Tin Tin

An all-American hero: war dog, film star, LEGEND. No relation to Tintin.

Chances are, if you love dogs as much as I do, that you already know everything there is to know about Rin Tin Tin, or Rinty to his friends. The iconic male German shepherd was a star on the battlefield, silver screen and radio, and in books and just about everything else he put his paws on.

Rescued from a French battlefield during World War One when he was only a few weeks old by American soldier Lee Duncan, Rin Tin Tin was smuggled back to the United States at the end of the war. Duncan believed that his new best friend was a good luck charm. He wasn't wrong! When back on home soil, Duncan and Rinty headed to the bright lights and glare of the Golden State, where Rinty managed to secure a few roles in some silent films. Rinty was to become an actor, a dog star that would burn brighter than Sirius.

It wasn't until 1923 – five years after Duncan had found him in a field in France – that Hollywood discovered Rinty and gave him his first big break, a leading role starring in the film *Where the North Begins*. According to legend, Rinty signed the contract for this movie with his paw-print! I can't imagine that's legally binding in any way, but it's fun to think it might be true.

The film was a huge hit and led to Rin Tin Tin taking up acting as a full-time job and between 1923 and 1932 he was never without work. He went on to star in twenty-seven (twenty-seven!!!) films and, according to some, the enduring appeal and blockbuster success of these films can be credited with bringing the famous Warner Bros. studio back from the brink of bankruptcy.

In 1929, the Oscars, or Academy Awards if you prefer, were awarded for the very first time, amidst the throng of the industry's most famous glitterati. According to a recent book about Rin Tin Tin by renowned writer Susan Orlean, the dog received the most votes for Best Actor. However, the Academy was keen to establish the Oscars as a serious affair and were understandably anxious about awarding a dog the very first, and most important, Oscar. In the end, Austrian actor Emil Jannings won for his role in the movie *The Way of All Flesh*.

 The poor dog, in life the firmest friend. The first to welcome, foremost to defend.

LORD BYRON

FORTUNÉ

Any dog that has an accént in its name is OK by mé and deserves to be called a super dog on that merit alone. But then, any dog that also bites Napoléon in his own bed, also deserves the title too, no questions asked.

Napoleon Bonaparte has always interested history academics. He was a fascinating fellow, a great strategic military leader, Emperor of France (a title he made up for himself, mind), instigator of the civil Napoleonic Code and, depending on which history book you read, a man of stature that was much smaller than his ego.

But, for one moment at least, let us put aside what we know about Napoleon. Let us instead concentrate on his first wife, Joséphine de Beauharnais, and more importantly, her pug super dog, Fortuné (pronounced *Fortun-neigh*).

Unlike her husband, de Beauharnais was a dog lover; a dog fanatic. She adored her Fortuné just as much, if not more, as her pug-like (small, fat and ugly) husband. Before de Beauharnais married Napoleon she allowed her pug to sleep in her bed, a custom that she would continue to allow – nay, insist upon – during her marriage, much to Napoleon's obvious annoyance. Alas, Napoleon never got a good night's rest when Fortuné the brave was around! In fact, it is recorded that Fortuné was so angry at having to share *his* bed, and de Beauharnais's affection, with the Emperor of France, that the

133

dog would sometimes bite Napoleon upon his entering the marital bed – an act that would send the leader of the nation into spasms of rage.

While I won't put the blame for the breakdown of de Beauharnais and Napoleon's marriage primarily on Fortuné's shoulders (de Beauharnais wrote later that it was her debts that drove them apart), I can't help but think that de Beauharnais's insistence on a *ménage-a-trois en chien* every night did their marriage no favours either!

So, let's raise a glass of champagne to Fortuné, the super dog who stopped Napoleon's conjugal relations with his beautiful wife. Not perhaps the most heroic of super-dog traits in the book, but one that is certainly very amusing!

 To his dog, every man is Napoleon; hence the constant popularity of dogs.

ALDOUS HUXLEY

HACHIKŌ

それは本当に素晴らしいで
す－どのような素敵な犬
この犬は－ super dog!

'Hachikō, the Akita' may sound like a line from one of the songs in *The Lion King*, but the story of Hachikō, a faithful golden-brown Akita, is actually Japan's most famous dog tale. Like Greyfriars Bobby, the loyal Skye terrier who spent fourteen years guarding the grave of his master fifty years earlier, Hachikō was a beautiful (a spitz breed originating from the Akita mountains of Japan) and dedicated doggy, whose love for his master went beyond the call of duty. In Japan – despite being very naughty doggies with strong temperaments – Akitas are a symbol of good health and a national reflection of loyalty.

In 1923, in the city of Odate, in the Akita prefecture of Japan (the popular breed of dogs that originated there is named after the area), lived a professor called Hidesaburō Ueno, who taught at Tokyo University, a short train ride away. At the end of each day, Hachikō – who sadly could not ride the train to work with Ueno – would meet and greet his owner at the nearby Shibuya Station and they'd walk home together. This daily routine happened for years and I'm sure was a highlight in both their days. Imagine being greeted at the train station by your dog, after a hard day's work and a cramped commute – it would be heaven!

One day, this routine suddenly changed. Professor Ueno never came home. He had died instantly from a brain

135

haemorrhage while at work. Hachikō's walk home was never to be the same again. However, that didn't stop him from going to the train station.

Every day for the next *nine years*, at the same time each afternoon, just as Professor Ueno's train continued to pull in, Hachikō would be seen walking up to the station, stopping and waiting. Waiting for the master who would never come. Hachikō never gave up hope that his master would one day appear at the station, so that they could continue their cherished walk home together. Sadly, it was not to be.

One day Hachikō's body was found near the station, the apparent victim of a stabbing, though it was later confirmed by autopsy that Hachikō had contracted cancer and had been deeply unwell. He was dead, but his loyalty had not been in vain. This super dog had acquired a loyal following of his own.

News of Hachikō's lengthy loyalty after his master's death had spread throughout the local towns and villages and in time Hachikō became a national hero, a symbol of loyalty, and every year, on 8 April – the day of his passing – commuters pay respectful tribute to Hachikō at the station where he would meet his old friend.

 Truly, I would not hang a dog by my will, much more a man who hath any honesty in him.

WILLIAM SHAKESPEARE

PETRA

One of the small screen's first, and most iconic, dogs, *Blue Peter*'s Petra got audiences' tails wagging and inspired many children around the country to want to own a dog when they grew up...

In the past half-century many dogs have appeared on television that have impressed, inspired and encouraged coos of love and happiness from millions of viewers. American viewers had Lassie and Hobo, the two iconic super doggies who forever bound energetically into shot like modern-day action heroes; doggy versions of Rambo!

British viewers had Petra – slightly more subdued than the gung-ho Lassie, perhaps, but also more real. The iconic *Blue Peter* dog became a national hero and a star in her own right, and her legacy continues to shine. To generations of dog lovers, Petra was the first dog that they had ever seen on TV – a true marvel, especially if you were unable to have a dog as a pet yourself.

Appearing on the BBC's flagship children's programme between 1962 and 1977, Petra, a female mongrel, was the very first *Blue Peter* pet, and is perhaps still one of the best-known TV dogs in the whole of Britain. Ask anyone who grew up in this era to name the first *Blue Peter* pet and everyone will answer 'Petra!'.

She is still the longest-serving *Blue Peter* pet, which is amazing considering the show has gone on to host a long list of other famous animals, including horses, cats, parrots, and tortoises, as well as over ten other doggy co-hosts. All of whom have become national heroes, too!

As with many aspects of TV, Petra was a manufactured idea, dreamed up by the producers of the programme as a pet for children who were not allowed to keep animals of their own at home. So thanks to the magic of television, during every episode children could tune in for an hour or so every weekday and feel as if they too had their own pet dog; it was a beautiful idea, and it is one that works successfully to this day.

Petra's rise to fame started off, as all good doggy tales do, with a tiny amount of tragedy. Only a few days after the first appearance of *Blue Peter*'s new dog co-host, the first dog the show's producers had chosen, the dog died abruptly of distemper. Not wanting to upset children over the disappearance of their new beloved doggy, the show's production team quickly scoured the country and found a dog-a-like at a pet shop in Lewisham... and the show went ahead without any children noticing the replacement. Viewers went on to name the puppy Petra in a competition, a competition that is still upheld to this day for new arrivals.

In September 1965, Petra gave birth to eight puppies, including Patch, who went on to become another of the show's co-hosts. Sadly, in 1977, Petra became ill and was retired from the programme. She was put down on 14 September 1977. Her passing was reported in the national press, one of the first dogs to have made such headlines.

Such was Petra's beloved status at the BBC – and around the country in general – that a statue of her was erected outside the prestigious Television Centre at Wood Lane in London. In 1984 it was moved to the famous *Blue Peter* garden. Petra was a true national icon and is still remembered today as one of the UK's first 'celebrity' dogs – a fact worth remembering the next time you type 'funny dog videos' on YouTube.

 Outside of a dog, a book is a man's best friend. Inside of a dog, it's too dark to read.

GROUCHO MARX

SUPER DOGS
OF ALL SORTS

Dogs come in all shapes and sizes, and the same can be said for super dogs. They come in different colours, varieties and breeds, and they come with different names; from the exotically named Xiao Sa to plain ol' Todd. Let's sneak-a-peek at a veritable feast of wonder dogs who have caught our attention in recent years…

XIAO SA

Chinese super dog star and Internet sensation, Xiao Sa (pronounced zow-ser) was just one of that country's millions of mongrel strays that dreamed of a new life. A true, and incredible, story of what happens when you give a super dog a bone...

In China, currently, there are a reported 130 million stray dogs – a number that is increasing, tragically, every single day. Due to the growing urbanisation being experienced in the country, many pet owners are beginning to abandon their animals on the streets when they take up residence in newer high-rise properties. These stray animals are left to fend for themselves on the busy and lonely streets, without food or proper shelter.

One such dog was a female white mongrel with one of the cutest faces you've ever seen. The dog didn't have a name, or at least nobody knew it. It was a wanderer, roaming from town to town sniffing out any morsels of scraps it could find.

Thankfully, that was to all change for the better one day in June 2012, when a cross-country cycling team passed through on a 3,000-mile ride from Kangding, Sichuan province, to Lhasa in Tibet. It was a cycle ride that tested human physical endurance and strength and it would push the entire team to their limits. There was little room for error. However, there was just enough room for a very little dog... with VERY big determination.

On that day, when the team stopped to take a rest off highway G318 on the Qinghai-Tibet plateau, one of the cyclists, a twenty-two-year-old student, Zhang Heng, spotted a little mutt lying tired and shaggy on the side of the street. Using a chicken drumstick from his own scarce rations, Zhang walked up to the dirty little ball of scruff and gave the dog a meal full of delicious meat and protein – just the type of food that would put a spring back in a dog's step.

As the cyclists prepared to continue their treacherous route, it seemed that they had picked up a new member on their team. Thankful for Zhang's kind act of simple generosity, the mutt had decided to run alongside his new best friend – and over the next 1,100 miles, until the end of their journey, the two became inseparable. Over the course of this feat of endurance, the previously unnamed dog became known as Xiao Sa, or 'Little Sa', Sa representing the last syllable of the cyclists' final destination, Lhasa. After months of being abandoned, unloved and nameless, Xiao Sa had a name, an identity and loads of new friends all looking out for her. During the marathon ride, the team and their new best friend rode and trotted respectively over mountains higher than 13,000 feet (4,000 m). Xiao Sa took it all in her stride; the long dusty roads and the steep climbs, running alongside the team for the entire journey, except for the steep downhill parts when the cyclists were building up too much speed for her to keep up – she was put in a basket on the front of the bike during these bits.

After a few days on the road with Xiao Sa, Zhang created a blog for his new-found pet, so that he could tell the world about this little dog with such determination. Very quickly the blog became an Internet sensation, with many thousands of followers, and with many local news outlets sending camera crews to report the story of Xiao Sa's incredible feat. Zhang declared his feelings for his fluffy friend to a local news team during the race, 'I have a special feeling about her, especially when I found she was never lost and waited for us at milestones on the road, and ran all the time, making me feel that she never feels tired!'

If you want to see this remarkable super dog in action, there are some fun videos and images online of the super scruffball with her little legs motoring under her tiny frame, tongue wagging, running alongside the cyclists. It is a sight to behold.

'I met Xiao Sa on the road, and she recognised me as a good friend and owner,' Zhang said after the ride. 'I won't leave her alone. I would like to take the dog home and take care of her. She has been a stray on the road for a long time. She needs a home.'

Zhang was true to his word. He flew his new friend back to Wuhan, where he was from, and since 2012 has given her a healthy, happy home full of love and affection and, hopefully, an unlimited supply of chicken drumsticks.

The story of Xiao Sa and Zhang Heng is a tale that beautifully demonstrates the deep bond and level of trust that can develop between a dog and a human, as well as the lengths they will go to, to ensure that bond never breaks.

If you pick up a starving dog and make him prosperous he will not bite you. This is the principal difference between a dog and man.

MARK TWAIN

TODD

As reported by the local and national press in a frenzy of brave doggy derring-do, it is now my privilege to tell the story of Todd the Labrador, who, after falling overboard one sunny afternoon, was considered lost at sea.

Everybody loves the doggy paddle. It's the first swimming stroke we all learn as children, but, let's face it, it's not the most attractive way of staying a float. But for one plucky swimmer, who risked his life trying to get home, doggy paddle worked wonders. This is the story of Todd, a very super swimming dog!

Picture the scene: it's a beautiful summer afternoon in July 2002. A family is enjoying some quality sun-tanning on board their boat. All is blissful with the world. The sun is shining and the family is at peace.

Until, that is, they suddenly realise that their pet dog, Todd, has gone missing. He is no longer on the boat. He is, in fact, not anywhere to be seen. The family starts to panic. They start to shout out to other boats. Peter Loizou, the head of the family, alarmed, sends out a radio message to nearby boat crews and anyone else who might help. This is a Mayday of dog-sized proportions. After four hours of searching the murky Solent waters, calling out for Todd until their voices were hoarse, the distressed family finally called off the search and headed towards the shore, towards home. The sun set, and night began to fall.

So where was Todd?

As it transpired – and as was reported for many weeks after the incident in many regional and national newspapers – after slipping overboard while snoozing on the front deck of the boat, a mile off the Isle of Wight, Todd had been left with no choice but to doggy-paddle to safety.

Todd could have opted to head for the nearest landmass, the Isle of Wight, but, instead, he navigated Britain's busiest waterway following his nose towards the mainland where the Loizou family, his owners, lived in the New Forest. It appears that Todd knew instinctively which way was home even if it meant taking the much longer route to safety. He managed to paddle his way through the channel, swimming right alongside ferries, tankers, ocean liners and sailboats, not to mention against strong currents, and ended up, dog-tired, on the mainland shore. Still heading for home on dry land, he was discovered by a teenager and her grandfather. Todd was promptly taken to a nearby vet, where his microchip identified his home address, and then was taken back home to his owners.

When Loizou returned home later that night, inconsolable at the loss of his furry friend, there was Todd waiting to greet him. I would have loved to see the look on his face. He must have been thinking, 'HOW ON EARTH DID YOU GET HERE?!'

Todd's doggy-paddle was an epic six-hour journey of self-discovery that covered an incredible 10 miles. Not only did he find out he was an amazing swimmer, he also found out that, when it comes to being lost at sea, it always pays to keep your head above water, keep calm and paddle on.

 A dog is the only thing on earth that loves you more than he loves himself.

JOSH BILLINGS

NIPPER

Nipper was famous locally in Bristol, England, because he liked nipping and biting the legs of visitors turning up at his owner's front door! However, his true everlasting fame was to arrive many years after his death...

In 1898, the brother of Nipper's original owner, Francis Barraud, painted a picture of Nipper looking quizzically down a brass phonograph, wondering where the sound was coming from.

In the late nineteenth century, gramophones, and the records they played, were still objects of intense wonder. Not many humans, let alone dogs, could afford to own one. Therefore, Nipper's expression and interest in the sound that was magically appearing from this fascinating instrument serves as a perfect representation of how people at the time felt about recorded music – this strange new invention that felt, looked and sounded like nothing anybody had ever touched, seen or heard before, and which would completely change the world.

That sense of wonder, *of listening to something new*, is how we all feel about music at some point in our lives, and it is this idea that caught the imagination of executives at HMV music, who opened their flagship store on Bond Street, London in 1921 with Nipper emblazoned on their front door – though this time Nipper was unable to bite the legs of any of the visitors! Much, I'm sure, to his disappointment.

The logo – a reworking of Barraud's original painting – remains to this day the HMV logo, even if the former heavyweights of the high street have struggled to keep going in tough economic times. After briefly going into administration in 2013, the iconic music retailer was bailed out by refinancing firm Hilco a few months later, meaning doors remain open for business for the foreseeable future.

The company's logo – especially the large-scale one adorning the Bond Street store entrance – will, hopefully, always stand as a tribute to a dog who received worldwide recognition as an icon of a changing world, and of progress, but who sadly never knew it.

 Just give me a comfortable couch, a dog, a good book and a woman.

GROUCHO MARX

WELLARD (OR KYTE)

For a brief period of my teenage life – when I was at my most impressionable – I was addicted to *EastEnders*. I think this addiction probably stemmed from the fact that the least annoying character on the programme was Wellard, the show's longest-serving pet...

Wellard, just like Schmeichel (Chesney Brown's Great Dane on ITV's *Coronation Street*, for those who don't know), is a true super dog of the modern era. Not only because of its TV-career longevity (envied by many of the human cast), but also because it had to put up with horrible on-screen owners who treated it badly. It also had to put up with some terrible acting and the hackneyed storylines that made for wincing viewing for the millions who tuned in every night. Addicted.

Wellard, or Kyte to its off-screen master and mates, was in fact a female Belgian Tervuren, a beautiful breed of shepherd dog with lovely pointy ears, a fluffy tail, a lionesque mane, a proud, almost regal, poise, and a tongue longer than a human arm. She first appeared on the misery-soap in 1994 and starred in most episodes up until 'his' death (on the show) in 2008.

Wellard was one of the show's longest-serving characters, making him 'well hard' indeed, for having put up with all the whingeing, and shouting, and fighting, and crying, and shouting, and whingeing, and crying, and fighting that he must have seen in all his years on the Square.

Wellard's owner, the eternally down-on-his-luck Robbie Jackson (played by the irreplaceable Dean Gaffney), was forever caught in the crossfire of some slanging or slagging match between Albert Square's fierce rivals, a sort of even more OTT version of the Montagues squaring off with the Capulets, only in east London, and with loads more dropped 'h's.

Wellard was killed off in 2008 after a storyline that saw him bite local cafe owner, Ian Beale. The audience didn't respond to the biting incident well and Wellard was eventually killed off after that 'silly cow' Bianca Jackson (played by Patsy Palmer) repeatedly fed Wellard too much chocolate – a big no-no, as any dog lover would know-know. After fourteen years of long service, Wellard died the most clichéd and pointless pet death ever to be witnessed before the watershed on British television.

The Jackson family reminisced about the good times they had shared with Wellard as the poor dog lay in the living room, struggling to breathe, and as the family and the audience awaited the expected knock on the door. Death arrived in the form of a vet, who was to put Wellard to sleep once the family had said their teary goodbyes. 'So long, Wellard, you mighty titan of Albert Square,' the audience cried at his tear-jerking final scene, watched by millions of the show's fans. Wellard had not only been an important member of the Jackson family, he had also become a vital member of the EastEnders cast.

During her tenure as Wellard, Kyte also notched up an impressive appearance in the 2000 blockbuster *Gladiator* as the loyal dog-soldier of Maximus (played by Russell Crowe).

 Dogs are not our whole life, but they make our lives whole.

ROGER A. CARAS

BOUNCER

Bouncer, the intrepid and handsome Labrador retriever from the incredibly popular, and enduring, Australian TV soap *Neighbours*. Bouncer was a super dog that ruled the daytime TV schedules and for six years was the most loved dog Down Under.

Many of the show's millions of fans loved, and still love, Bouncer. For many, Bouncer's storylines were more interesting than those of the other characters appearing in *Neighbours* at the time. In fact, to many viewers, myself included, Bouncer was a better actor than even the future household names that starred in the show.

Bouncer's seven-year stint on the show, from 1987 to 1993, included the exalted and overly celebrated wedding of Kylie Minogue's Charlene to Jason Donovan's Scott – a storyline that climaxed with over 20 million viewers and, according to some, changed popular culture forever.

However, what I liked about Bouncer, more than anything else, was that he wasn't playing a character called Bouncer. His actual name was Bouncer. I don't see the point in TV dogs being called something different than their own name, unless it suits the character (as we have seen, Wellard from *EastEnders* was meant to be 'well hard', but was actually played by a dog called Kyte). But what's the point of calling Bouncer 'Jimbo', for example, when Bouncer is perfect as it is.

SUPER DOGS OF ALL SORTS

Bouncer's original owner in the show was Mike Young (played by Guy Pearce, now a Hollywood superstar), who gave Bouncer to Lucy Robinson (played by Melissa Bell, not a Hollywood superstar and therefore able to become a regular on the show). Bouncer played a huge part in quite a few arresting storylines, including becoming Ramsay Street's number one hero when he saved Madge Bishop from a chip pan fire by barking loudly for help. Obviously – and you can't discuss Bouncer without mentioning this – the most controversial storyline, perhaps on the show ever, involved Bouncer's disastrous 'dream sequence', which saw Bouncer dream that he was marrying Rosie, a sheepdog that lived next door and belonged to Clarrie McLachlan (Frederick Parslow). The dream sequence has become one of the programme's defining moments, and perhaps one of TV's all-time memorable scenes, even if you might argue that the writers' sense of writing fun dog storylines got the better of them. It was also the first, and so far only, time a character dog appearing on television ever had its own dream sequence.

Three months after retiring from the show, in 1993, Bouncer died of cancer. Following his death, Bouncer's trainer and owner, Luke Hara, received hundreds of thousands of tributes from distraught fans. Readers of Britain's *TV Magazine* voted Bouncer the third-favourite soap dog of all time.

 The greatest pleasure of a dog is that you may make a fool of yourself with him, and not only will he not scold you, but he will make a fool of himself, too.

SAMUEL BUTLER

PICKLES

England may have won the football World Cup in 1966 but, if it hadn't been for Pickles, the team may have won nothing at all...

In the summer of 1966 England won the football World Cup – the gleaming Jules Rimet trophy – on home soil. The entire nation celebrated for days. You could argue we're still celebrating it now! To England football fans, winning the final on that beautiful day almost fifty years ago wasn't *just* about winning a football trophy that was primarily important to eleven men in shorts. No, winning the Jules Rimet signified something more important; it was a victory that reminded the world that England – having been on the brink of destruction only twenty-six years earlier – was still powerful, a nation to take seriously, even if it was only on a football pitch.

So, when the Jules Rimet trophy – the future symbol of England's moment of sporting glory – went missing on 20 March, just four months before the World Cup was due to be played, things could have become quite embarrassing for the English, not just at home, but everywhere around the world. Imagine the shame of losing one of the most precious sporting awards in the world before a major international tournament to be played in your own back yard? If it were never found, we would have never lived it down.

Thank god for Pickles, then. Pickles, the metaphorical bulldog who was, in fact, a black and white collie.

On the afternoon of Sunday 20 March, the trophy – valued at around £3,000 in 1966, (around £45,000 in today's money) – was being displayed at an exhibition of rare stamps at Westminster Central Hall in London, when a burglar (no doubt carrying a bag with the word 'SWAG' on it – it was the sixties, after all) half-inched the trophy from under the noses of everybody in the room. None of the guards protecting the trophy had noticed anything suspicious, until the trophy was gone. While the very real Pink Panther cleverly managed to steal the Jules Rimet, however, he was perhaps too stupid to realise that the rare stamps were worth far more – almost £3 million more, in fact! Later that day, the Metropolitan Police at Scotland Yard took control of the operation to retrieve the trophy. The next day, they received a £15,000 (roughly £225,000 in today's money) ransom demand, to be paid in £1 and £5 notes. When the police apprehended the culprit the following day, it turned out that he was a hoaxer who had demanded a ransom as a joke. For the next seven days, the police, the public and, no doubt, the national football team lived on a knife's edge.

Thankfully – and yet rather bizarrely – the trophy was found a week later, seemingly out of the blue. David Corbett and his dog Pickles had been out for a walk around Beulah Hill in south-east London, when on the way home Pickles suddenly began to sniff curiously at a parcel concealed under a hedge near Corbett's house. It was wrapped in an old newspaper and tied with string. When Corbett opened the parcel, he recognised the trophy and immediately handed it in at his local police station in Gypsy Hill. To say the police were rather suspicious of Mr Corbett – and Pickles – was an understatement, but they could never prove any foul play.

The next morning the police announced the recovery of the trophy and it was returned to the Football Association, who were in charge of organising the World Cup tournament. As a reward for Pickles's important discovery he was invited to a fancy celebration banquet, where he was treated as a very special VIP indeed. He was even allowed to lick Corbett's dessert bowl. In fact, for months following England's stunning victory at Wembley, Pickles became something of a celebrity for many people. Football fans and dog lovers alike turned up at Corbett's front door to shake the paw of the dog that had saved England's bacon. Corbett collected a £6,000 reward (about £90,000 in today's money, so not a bad day's work), but the actual thief was never caught*.

Sadly, Pickles died in 1967 when he choked on his leash while chasing a cat. He was buried in Corbett's back garden and his collar went on display in the National Football Museum in Manchester. If you're ever in that neck of the woods, and fancy paying tribute to a dog that helped win the World Cup, it's well worth popping in to see.

 In times of joy, all of us wished we possessed a tail we could wag.

W. H. AUDEN

---

* As an addendum to this story, the Jules Rimet trophy was stolen again, in Brazil in 1983 (it had been given to Brazil in perpetuity after they won the World Cup for a third time in 1970). But this time it was never recovered.

CHASER

Dogs are often ignorantly called 'stupid', though usually only by stupid and ignorant people. Dogs are anything but stupid, and Chaser is the proof in the pudding. He is the Smartest Dog in the World.

If you're the owner of a fairly average dog, you'll know that your dog can pretty much only understand and respond to a few basic commands. 'Sit', 'paw' and 'other paw' are three that I think most dogs (sort of) understand. But, if you want to know about the Smartest Dog in the World, then look no further than Chaser. This black and white (or 'cookies and cream', as described by her owner) Border collie from South Carolina, USA is a truly geeky dog with a very high IQ.

In fact, Chaser is so smart she is often described as the dog with the largest tested memory of any animal on the planet, as well as having the largest vocabulary of any animal *ever*. Chaser is even smarter than the smartest monkey in the world, Kanzi, who is believed to currently understand around 450 words. So, why is Chaser so smart?

Well, for a start, she can identify the names of more than 1,000 toys and objects, and is able to retrieve them from a pile of other items and toys, as well as categorise them by function or shape – a trait that a human child develops at around three years old. But Chaser can do more than that

– she isn't just learning objects by name, *she's beginning to understand the basic structure of human language.* Chaser cannot only understand words like 'hot' and 'cold', but also the difference between the two. She knows over 1,200 words – and not just nouns, but verbs too, and even some adjectives and prepositions!

Psychologists Dr John Pilley and Dr Alliston Reid have been intensively training Chaser to identify objects for many years. Their teaching techniques are built on the evolutionary model for learning and classical conditioning developed, as we have seen, by Ivan Pavlov (see chapter headed 'Pavlov's Dogs'). Chaser has been educated not just about words, but also about the constructs of language, and without requiring food as a reward; this dog is fulfilled by the task itself.

So what is the secret to this remarkable success? Pilley puts it down to teaching Chaser verbs first, such as 'drag', 'beg' or 'fetch'. Verbs were picked up more quickly by her than nouns, as a dog doesn't understand names as quickly as it can understand actions. Pilley noted in his research that when it came to learning and, more importantly, understanding words, Chaser was first taught words that were of value to her ('eat', 'run', 'walk'), as opposed to just random names of items. Once Chaser understood the importance of the actions being expressed, the learning of abstract nouns was simplified.

Chaser's progress does beg the question of whether success is down to the intensive teaching, or whether she is simply a very intelligent Border collie – without doubt one of the smartest breeds of dog in the first place. It's difficult to say, though we'd all like to think it's a bit of both. Anyone who has ever met a Border collie knows that they are whip-smart animals, even without intensive teaching.

Chaser's first book, *Chaser: Unlocking the Genius of the Dog Who Knows a Thousand Words*, was published in 2013, though it was, disappointingly, written by Pilley and not Chaser herself! For anyone fascinated with the subject of dog training, the book is thoroughly recommended, but don't expect it to give you all the answers when it comes to understanding why your dog still can't 'sit' after eleven years of trying!

 After years of having a dog, you know him. You know the meaning of his snuffs and grunts and barks.

ROBERT R. McCAMMON

SNUPPY

First there was Dolly the sheep, the first cloned animal, named after the buxom singer Dolly Parton. Now there is Snuppy the puppy, the first cloned dog. A super dog of the twenty-first century...

Cloning is an ethical, political and social hot potato. It's one of those issues that tend to send people with strong opinions into a tizzy. Whatever your opinion, it's difficult to deny that the idea of the first cloned dog begs an intriguing question: Will there one day be an army of cloned super dogs? Let's hope so, but let's also hope that they'll be on our side and not that of the machines!

Anyway, let's meet pup of the month, Snuppy – the first cloned dog to survive birth. This first-of-a-kind Afghan hound was created by biomedical scientist Hwang Woo-Suk and his team of scientists at Seoul National University (SNU) in South Korea. Unlike Dolly the sheep being named after the singer Dolly Parton (Dolly was cloned from a mammary gland, you see), Snuppy's name is not quite so snappy – his name is a portmanteau of puppy and SNU, the acronym of Seoul National University. But I'm sure you had worked that out already!

Snuppy's cellular growth was stimulated when a donor egg cell was fused with DNA from the ear of Tie, a three-year-old male Afghan hound, before being transferred to a surrogate golden Labrador female (over 120 surrogate mothers were implanted, but only Snuppy survived) for a full sixty days of pregnancy. Snuppy was born on 25 April 2005 by Caesarean section and his birth made headlines around the world.

While this story may sound like a lot of scientists playing God (or playing Dog, if you fancy), and there are, obviously, certain ethical elements to ponder, I can't help but think that Snuppy is a miracle of science, a true clone. He was the dog that made it, that survived, and he is now living a healthy and happy life. He has also been used in the first known successful breeding between two cloned dogs! Snuppy's sperm was used to artificially inseminate two cloned females which, I'm happy to report, resulted in the birth of ten bouncing puppies in 2008.

So, there we have it! The first cloned dog and the first cloned baby dog with two cloned parents! I wonder what science will give us next.

 A dog is not considered a good dog because he is a good barker. A man is not considered a good man because he is a good talker.

BUDDHA

Boo

Boo, the World's Cutest Dog, has in recent years surprised the 'social petworking' world into a palpable frenzy of adorable delirium. Published 'author', airline spokesdog, Internet sensation and over 12 million 'likes' on Facebook; the world is Boo's oyster!

I imagine you haven't been hiding under a rock for the past five years, but even if you have been, you may still have heard of Boo, possibly the Internet's most popular dog. The world has always been dog-crazy but, with the spread of the Internet, dog-sharing online has become one of the Zeitgeisty things of the twenty-first century. And sitting politely and very adorably at the centre of this digital maelstrom is Boo – a dog too impossibly cute for words – but I'll do my best.

Boo, a cuddly ball of energetic Pomeranian, known for his trademark hairstyle – basically, he looks like a fluffy snowball – was born on 16 March 2006. Boo belongs to Irene Ahn, a San Francisco resident and senior Facebook executive, who first created a Facebook page to let the dog introduce himself, announcing proudly to the world: 'My name is Boo. I am a dog. Life is good.' Boo found fame and an element of notoriety in October 2010 when a few celebrity dog-admirers, including celebrity socialite (that's a thing, right?) Khloé Kardashian, called Boo the 'cutest dog on the planet'. From there on, things just started to snowball for the dog. And within a few months the world had gone Boo-mad. Many cynics claim the success of Boo was an 'inside job' by Facebook (Boo has over 12 million likes) in order to promote the site and shift the slew of merchandise, including Boo's first record-breaking book.

Written under Ahn's nom de plume, J. H. Lee, *Boo: The Adventures of the Cutest Dog in the World* was published to great commercial acclaim and translated into ten languages and counting. It has already sold over two million copies. Ahn went to great lengths to ensure she was never associated publicly with Boo's success and claims she only posted pictures of her punky Pomeranian to Facebook 'for laughs'.

Following the success of the book, a vast array of Boo-related merchandise hit the shelves, including a second book, *Boo: Little Dog in the Big City*, calendars, T-shirts, mugs, cuddly plush toys and, no doubt soon to follow, theme parks and world domination. For all we know Boo may become a great dog of grand stature, as important as other super dogs of his generation. But for now, let us all bask in Boo's unprecedented glory as 'spokesdog' for Virgin America, where, in 2012, he was named the Official Pet Liaison of the airline. Don't worry, I'm not sure what that means either.

Here's to Boo – a very modern model of a major model celebrity!

 There are things you get from the silent devoted companionship of a dog that you can get from no other source.

DORIS DAY

NORMAN

Dogs love to scoot – every dog lover knows this. But Norman the Scooter Dog loves an entirely different type of 'scoot'. Prepare to be amazed!

We humans love to embarrass our dogs: we dress them up in fancy costumes; we parade them all quaffed and buffed in front of silly judges with clipboards; we get them to do all sorts of ridiculous and pointless things, like jump through hoops and run around posts for our entertainment, when all they want to do is lie in their comfy beds and dream sweet meaty dreams of being fed tasty scraps at the dining room table.

But there are some dogs who take to these ridiculous requests of ours like metaphorical ducks to water and embarrass us right back at how untalented we are by comparison. Take Norman, for example. He's a super dog. Of that there is no doubt. He's a super dog that, in 2013, was awarded a *Guinness World Record*... for riding a scooter!

Norman the Scooter Dog, as he is known and loved, is a talented French sheepdog who has been officially verified by *Guinness World Records* as the fastest dog on a scooter, after travelling 100 feet (30 metres) in just over 20 seconds.

Let's imagine the scene on the day that Norman scooted into the record books: a big hairy sheepdog, his front paws on the handlebars, his back legs upright as if he were just a regular human about to casually go scootering. It's pretty incredible considering dogs are a) not bipedal; b) have no concept of what 'scootering' is; and c) see a).

Norman's record-breaking scootering attempt was captured by the American news programme *Today*, and shows, well, a dog on its two back legs scootering across a basketball court as if it were the most natural thing in the world. Norman's proud owner, Karen Cobb, claimed, 'He picked it up really quickly when he was a puppy and then just became comfortable around everyday human objects.'

Apparently, when he first noticed people scootering around him on the streets outside of his house, he wanted to be involved and that's when he got his paws on the scooter. 'He loved it. He wouldn't get off,' Cobb continued.

And, in case you were wondering, yes, Norman is also capable of riding a skateboard and a bike with training wheels, but has not yet broken the world record for those. Pretty soon we'll see Norman doing Evel Knievel-type stunts, perhaps some loop-de-loops through rings of fire while dancing on a motorcycle. At least I hope so…

A dog reflects the family life. Whoever saw a frisky dog in a gloomy family, or a sad dog in a happy one? Snarling people have snarling dogs, dangerous people have dangerous ones.

SIR ARTHUR CONAN DOYLE

CRAB

Crab the dog. This 'cruel-hearted cur' was the beloved dog of Launce and appeared in William Shakespeare's first ever play, *The Two Gentlemen of Verona*, believed to have been written between 1589 and 1592.

Despite Shakespeare coining the word 'watchdog', Crab was the only dog to appear as a character in any play by the Bard. Crab's character was, of course, a scene-stealer and, according to his master, the jester-servant Launce, 'I think Crab, my dog, be the sourest-natured dog that lives.' When Launce announces that he is to move away from his family due to his work with his master Proteus, his family are heartbroken, but Crab doesn't seem that bothered. As Launce recounts: 'yet did not this cruel-hearted cur shed one tear: he is a stone, a very pebble stone and has no more pity in him than a dog.'

Unlike Argos, Odysseus's very faithful dog in Homer's *Odyssey*, Crab is not at all sad that his master is leaving, but the audience is given no indication of Crab's emotional state. Shakespeare, it seemed, wanted Crab to be his own character – unlike Launce himself, who is very much the faithful dog to his own master, Proteus. Having an unloyal dog to a very loyal human master was perhaps just too much of a comical opportunity to miss, especially when compared to the other, more serious, relationships that occur in the play.

Crab and Launce's friendship is the comic foil the play requires to offset the contemplative relationship between the Duke and Proteus. Certainly this seems to be the case in Act IV, Scene IV, when Crab gets caught taking 'a pissing' on the floor, while underneath the table. Launce, forever the loyal servant, springs to Crab's defence and takes the blame for it. He also takes a beating and endures public humiliation. While this scene may have titillated the audience of Shakespeare's age, the scene ends with the public beating of a character the audience is supposed to love. All very Shakespearean, you may think – he never allows us to enjoy the moment for too long.

This humorous, yet pivotal, scene is intimated in the film *Shakespeare in Love* – written by another master playwright, Tom Stoppard. In the film, Queen Elizabeth gleefully recounts in a wicked one-liner that her favourite part from Shakespeare's new play is 'the bit with the dog', clearly referring to Act IV, Scene IV. The Queen gives an insight into how dogs, and in particular dog-related comedy slapstick and mishap, were often used during the sixteenth century as a simple, but effective, way to raise a laugh in the audience, especially at the royal court (for whom Shakespeare was paid to write many of his plays), where the audience was particularly hard to please.

Crab was a brilliant character creation that played against the typical man and faithful dog cliché, which is both humorous and thought-provoking.

Suffice to say that Crab is a super dog for not only being the only dog in any Shakespeare play, but also for not being a stereotypical dog; Crab is a super dog with a difference.

 Dogs are better than human beings because they know but do not tell.

EMILY DICKINSON

RICOCHET

The world is full of new, and unique, types of super dogs. Meet Ricochet, 'the internationally renowned, award-winning surf dog who participates in surfing contests and, most importantly... SURFS WITH PURPOSE!'

Ricochet, or Ricki for short, is one of the very few dogs in the world that is also a professional surfer, and who, according to his dogtastic website, 'typically places in the top three in international surf dog contests'.

But Ricochet, a beautiful, brown, shaggy golden retriever, is more than just a surf dog. She is also a registered and certified therapy dog, and the only known dog in the world who surfs with special-needs children and people with disabilities as an assistive aid and SURFice dog. She has won several top dog awards, including the American Humane Association Hero Dog Award and Dog of the Year from the American Society for the Prevention of Cruelty to Animals (ASPCA).

Born in 2008, Ricki's biography reads like a tale of a puppy having an identity crisis. She was simply too full of energy and life to settle down and get a real job; a proper surf bum, then! Born and bred from birth to be a service dog, it seems Ricki simply just did not 'take' to the discipline and training required to fit the bill. Her heart was too set on being a surfing dog, instead.

With the help and support of some friends, she was entered as a puppy novice into the Purina Incredible Dog Challenge Surf Competition in 2009, and came third. Ricki had found her true calling. A calling that has not only changed her life for the better, but also the thousands of other lives that have benefited from her talent, not only as a surfer but also as a dedicated fundraiser for many charitable causes. In the past two years, she has raised over $300,000 for selected human and animal causes and hopes to raise much more in the future with her surfing skills.

Ricochet's YouTube videos, which have gone viral to millions, show our delightful doggy catching waves, *properly surfing*, and generally being a proper beach bum.

 Properly trained, a man can be dog's best friend.

COREY FORD

Epicyon

> Neither a dog that you would want to cuddle, nor a dog that you would want sitting on your lap; Epicyon was a great big beast of a creature that would give anyone nightmares.

Epicyon, pronounced *epp-ih-sigh-on*, meaning 'more than a dog', was a species of very large dog that existed in the last Miocene period, some 20 million years ago. This species of canid is a very distant ancestor of the modern domesticated dog, due to its super-massive dome-shaped forehead and powerful jaws, or 'enlarged lower fourth molar', to be precise. They were at one point one of the dominant species of the earth, dining at the top level of the food chain. The top dog.

At around 5 feet (1.52 metres) long and weighing the same as a brown bear, approximately 150 lbs (68 kilos), the Epicyon had a head like a large lion and was an instinctive scavenger, eating only the rotting meat and flesh of dead animals and carcasses. Historians believe that the Epicyon was the largest dog that ever lived – and it will probably remain so unless Freddy the Great Dane gets *really big* (see chapter headed 'Freddy').

Belonging to the subfamily Borophaginae ('bone-crushing dogs') of the canid genus, Epicyon fossils have been discovered all over the North American states, from Florida to California and even into Canada. Fossil experts believe they were around for 15 million years, meaning this beast of a dog liked to travel far and wide, and it no doubt ruled whatever land it wandered on to.

It is believed that all of today's modern dogs originate from this species that dominated the North American plains all those years ago, but it is unknown why this powerful predator became extinct. Some historians believe it was due to a lack of prey – once they had eliminated their food source, Epicyon was unable to snack on vegetation, and may even have turned to cannibalism. If only they had eaten fruit and vegetables, they'd still be around today. Which is a terrifying thought.

 The most affectionate creature in the world is a wet dog.

AMBROSE BIERCE

ROBOT

In the summer of 1940, a lost dog with a futuristic name went down to the woods and got a very big surprise...

During the early part of World War Two, when battle was raging in the French hillsides, five friends and a dog went hunting in the woods of the southern region of Dordogne. The dog, called Robot, a white terrier with a brown patch over his left eye, ran ahead of the boys – his hunting instinct and acute sense of smell getting the better of him, he was unable to control himself amidst the fun to be had within the forest. Too many trees! Too many leaves! Too many sticks! Too many holes! Wait. Holes?

Yes, Robot had discovered a hole.

As the boys shouted 'Robot!' as they tried to catch up with their dog, they suddenly realised he had disappeared, vanished into thin air. When Robot finally responded to the boys' calls with a bark, all they could hear was a muffled sound coming from below their feet. Had Robot gone underground?

Indeed, Robot had. Deep underground.

But Robot hadn't simply uncovered a hole and fallen down it (i.e. as with typical dog behaviour). He had revealed a doorway. A doorway to another world, a doorway to the magical past.

Robot had discovered the Lascaux Caves, one of the most important archaeological finds in recent history, and certainly the most important archaeological site ever found by a dog!

The Lascaux Caves, hidden deep below Lascaux Manor in south-west France, contained a treasure trove of prehistoric art, dating back a whopping 20,000 years. These sophisticated and complex cave drawings of men, horses, trees and deer went beyond anything else seen in the region's many other caves.

What Robot had discovered, along with his young friends, was the beginning of a prehistoric art revolution, never before seen by modern prehistoric art experts. These drawings opened up a world of debate and theory about who drew them, and why, and where they had come from. They offered clues about our ancestors and how they lived several millennia ago.

Robot hadn't just discovered a load of old art on the walls, or a bunch of prehistoric graffiti, he had uncovered one of the oldest set of drawings in the history of human evolution.

Next time you can't be bothered to take your dog out for a walk in the local woods, preferring to simply take them around the block, think twice – you never know where their nose may lead you!

 Dogs are wise. They crawl away into a quiet corner and lick their wounds and do not rejoin the world until they are whole once more.

AGATHA CHRISTIE

MARLEY

Those of you who have read *Marley and Me* will know that Marley was not a bad dog, just very misunderstood. But when Marley wasn't ruining the furniture or weeing on stuff, he was bringing his family closer together than they could have ever imagined.

Before the 2008 film starring Jennifer Aniston and Owen Wilson, there was the book. *Marley and Me*, published in 2005, told the autobiographical dog tale of journalist John Grogan and his dog, Marley, a bouldering, blundering and boisterous yellow Labrador retriever. He was named after the reggae singer Bob Marley, so beloved by his owner. Grogan had bought Marley as a pup from a local Labrador breeder for 350 dollars, but he grew up to be a 97-pound (44-kilo) steamroller of a dog!

The book began its life as a series of weekly columns Grogan wrote to highlight the fun, frolics and frustrations to be had bringing up a growing puppy in an already overcrowded New York City. As Grogan went from being a bachelor living alone to being a married man sharing a small apartment with a baby on the way, Marley at times proved a welcome companion and distraction, providing masses of love and affection at the end of a stressful day at work – as so many Labradors do – but at other times he put a strain on his master's burgeoning relationship.

Marley was always in trouble; always in the doghouse. Too big to control, and too big-hearted to warrant discipline, Marley was just Marley. Like some people, some dogs just walk their own path. The way Grogan discusses Marley's behaviour will ring true with many dog owners, no matter what breed they own. Marley's endless search for food, his tireless pursuit of activity and games at inappropriate moments, and his need to be played with or cuddled 24/7, became overbearing and difficult to manage in a growing family home, where babies, jobs and money stresses, not to mention expensive furniture, can constantly get in the way. Grogan's weekly column, and by extension his book, brilliantly captured the perils and pitfalls of having a dog as part of your family, especially the part about dogs always stealing and eating your wife's knickers or leaving huge amounts of dog slobber on freshly cleaned and ironed clothing!

Whenever Marley acted up, broke something or stole something, Grogan would describe Marley's 'mambo' – a little wriggle he would do that gave away his secret, a tell-tale sign.

There are these wonderful videos on YouTube of a yellow Labrador called Denver the Guilty Dog – which you must check out – a dog that whenever it is caught doing something naughty has the guiltiest face ever. It's as if Labradors know they are being naughty and can't help themselves, but have the honour and dignity to show they feel bad about it. Like Marley, Denver the Guilty Dog has clocked up millions of views – suggesting that there are a lot of sympathetic dog owners out there who connect with these naughty dogs who can't help getting into trouble. It was as if Marley's OTT zest for life was uncontainable, that nothing could stop him from having fun, not even screen doors or drywalls or obedience school, from which Marley was thrown out for being 'too playful'.

When Marley finally passed away, the reader learns that Marley's lifelong erratic behaviour had possibly been due to a condition, an illness that had affected his stomach. When Grogan wrote about the death of his dog in his newspaper column, concluding the journey that he had been on for thirteen years, the response from his readers was phenomenal. Marley – and his adorably MASSIVE personality – had become a true super dog in the minds of millions of weekly readers, thanks in part to the kind and honest words of his friend and master.

Dogs are great. Bad dogs, if you can really call them that, are perhaps the greatest of them all.

JOHN GROGAN

BOBBIE

Have you heard of Bobbie the Wonder Dog? This story – which became a national sensation in Prohibition-era America – will make you smile as wide as Bobbie's journey...

The year is 1923. The Brazier family were on a road trip, holidaying blissfully in Indiana, USA when their beloved dog – a two-year-old Scottish collie-mix named Bobbie – became lost from Mr and Mrs Brazier and their children. The family spent hours searching for him, perhaps hoping that he would spontaneously jump through some bushes, barking with joy at having won an extended game of Hide and Seek. Alas, he didn't, and the heartbroken family eventually resigned themselves to travelling the 2,800 miles back to their home in Silverton, Oregon without their furriest member of the family, believing they would never see him again. Six long months passed, Christmas came and went. The devastated Braziers had no choice but to move on.

It wasn't until February 1924, on a Wednesday, that something miraculous happened. When Mr Brazier woke up and opened his front door to pick up the morning newspapers, he almost stumbled over a dog in his front garden. It was a very mangy, scrawny and exhausted-looking dog. A dog whose feet were quite literally worn down to the bone and bleeding. A dog that looked a lot like their beloved Bobbie.

It was Bobbie!

The Braziers could not believe their eyes.

Against all odds, Bobbie had run, walked and staggered the 2,800-mile cross-country trek – in the dead of winter – from Indiana to Oregon to end up back home safe and sound with his family. How had he done it? Was it even possible? *Was it a miracle?* The Braziers didn't care – they were relieved and super-excited just to have their beautiful dog home with them.

And so was the rest of the town. News quickly spread of Bobbie's astonishing return and within days the local newspaper, the *Silverton Appeal Tribune,* published the story of Bobbie's amazing journey. Within a few weeks, Bobbie had become a national sensation, his story uplifting the souls of the American public. Many people wrote to the Brazier family, claiming they had seen a Bobbie-like dog wandering wearily through their town and were able to identify him through his distinctive marks. The Oregon Humane Society launched an investigation into Bobbie's trek and confirmed satisfactorily that he had in fact made the journey back home. *It was a miracle!* From then onwards the Braziers' dog was no longer simply Bobbie – he had become BOBBIE THE WONDER DOG!

For his extraordinary adventures, Bobbie received the prestigious Key to the City of Portland and a jewel-studded harness and collar. He was the guest of honour at the Portland Home Show – an event in which 40,000 people turned up just to see him. One fan even presented Bobbie with his own dog-sized bungalow to live in! Bobbie had become a national hero and celebrity, but also a symbol of hope and courage at a time when America was plunging headfirst into the Great Depression.

Though his momentous journey to see his family again almost cost him his life, and to this day no one is quite sure just how he managed to navigate his way home, Bobbie's health returned and he lived a glorious life with his family right up until his passing in 1927. *What a story!*

 If I could be half the person my dog is,
I'd be twice the human I am.

CHARLES YU

INDIANA

As a child, aspiring filmmaker George Lucas owned a friendly and adventurous dog: a beautiful Alaskan Malamute named Indiana. This dog inspired the creation of two – yes, two! – of the world's greatest ever movie characters on the big screen.

Firstly, it was the inspirational name for Lucas's daring and courageous Indiana Jones. Secondly, it was the imaginative inspiration behind one of Lucas's other great characters, Chewbacca, from the blockbusting *Star Wars* films.

Chewbacca is a gentle, hairy, non-English-speaking co-pilot that's 9 feet (2.7 metres) tall, is covered in fur, and carries a crossbow that fires lasers. It was inspired by Lucas's fascination at watching Indiana the dog sitting up in the passenger seat of his parents' car – as if he were a part of the family, a human, wanting to drive. This was when Lucas was growing up in the small town of Modesto, California – 2,300 miles away from the state of Indiana, from which the name most popularly derives.

Lucas even described the character of Chewbacca, a Wookiee from the planet Kashyyyk, as having been based on Indiana's looks, and, no doubt, smell. 'Indiana was the prototype for the Wookiee. He always sat beside me in the car. He was big, a big bear of a dog,' Lucas has said of his beloved pet.

And here's a fact you may not have known before: the word 'Chewbacca' is actually derived from the Russian word for dog, *собака* (cobaka). When the *Star Wars* 'sequels' hit the big screens in 2015 – unarguably the most anticipated film release in the history of cinema – take a seat in the front row and growl Chewbacca-style very loudly in Indiana's very super-special honour.

 Once you have had a wonderful dog, a life without one is a life diminished.

DEAN KOONTZ

TUNA

The Internet's most recent canine celebrity melts the heart of every dog lover – a chiweenie who really has to be seen to be believed. But this isn't just a flash-in-the-pan celebrity crush, no, Tuna's a one-of-a-kind super dog; a very rare breed indeed.

Over the past ten years there have been hundreds of wild, beautiful and courageous dogs online that have melted our hearts. In fact, it seems that not a day goes past without a new YouTube video of a wonderful doggy doing a unique dance or bark, or baking waffles, on the way to becoming a worldwide sensation. But the real star out of all these dogs, certainly for the foreseeable future, has to be the awesome, the spectacular, the ever-so-slightly eccentric Tuna.

This chihuahua-dachshund mix, or chiweenie, as they are adorably known, has an 'aggressive overbite, a lower recessed jawline, a crumpled chin, and a neck that looks like he has been soaking in the bathtub for days' (his owner's words, not mine!). It is the Internet's biggest (but also smallest) celebrity dog – or doglebrity, as I am coining them.

With over 750,000 followers on the photography-based social media network Instagram, and a veritable buffet of merchandise and products (including a coffee mug, iPhone case, T-shirt, apron and buttons!) with his name and face on, Tuna looks set to become a truly internationally famous superstar who has to be seen to be appreciated.

Tuna's Instagram account, www.instagram.com/tunameltsmyheart, posts a plethora of adorable photographs of Tuna with his famous teeth, eyes and smile melting your heart with each addictive daily view. As Tuna himself says, 'If you could use a little bit of joy and laughter, you've come to the right place!'

Tuna proves that, even in this age of celebrity-obsessed superficiality, beauty is only skin deep. His appearance is his strength, not his weakness, or, as his website declares: 'Those who see past Tuna's irregularities also adore him for them. They have eyes that see his true beauty, because true beauty captivates our hearts and not just our eyes.' Well said!

Tuna's owner, Courtney Dasher, adopted this unique chiweenie in 2011 and started posting pictures of him daily to a quickly growing fan base that soon became obsessed, desperate to see more and more images of Tuna's unconventionally cute face.

Tuna's early life began in heartbreaking circumstances, having been discarded by his previous owners on the side of a road in San Francisco, California when he was just a four-month-old puppy. Thankfully, Courtney found him at a local farmers' market and instantly fell in love with the little mite who quickly became her new best friend and has not left her side since. 'I would never have imagined that a little unwanted dog could have this much of an impression on people by bringing them so much joy and laughter,' Courtney wrote on her Tuna-related website. 'But then again, he is not your average dog.'

Tuna had found a loving home. But also, Courtney had found a loving dog, and their friendship is a testament to the fact that love can be found in the unlikeliest of locations and that beauty is truly in the eye of the beholder.

 Let sleeping dogs lie.

CHARLES DICKENS

ACKNOWLEDGEMENTS

My sincere thanks and gratitude must go to my publisher Claire Plimmer, editor Sophie Martin, and the rest of the brilliant Summersdale team, for all their hard work and all-round loveliness. Thanks also to Rachel Morland for her frequent cups of tea.

 A dog will teach you unconditional love. If you can have that in your life, things won't be too bad.

ROBERT WAGNER

ABOUT THE AUTHOR

Malcolm Croft is dog-mad. His adventurous two-year-old dachshund, Scooby, is quite simply the greatest thing on four legs and was the inspiration for *Super Dogs*.

When he is not cuddling Scooby, Malcolm is a writer and freelance editor specialising in non-fiction, and a former Commissioning Editor at a London publishing house. He has been in the publishing industry for over ten years and is the author of several popular non-fiction books.

 When a man's best friend is his dog, that dog has a problem.

EDWARD ABBEY

The
DOG LOVER'S
Digest

Vicky Barkes

THE DOG LOVER'S DIGEST

Vicky Barkes

ISBN: 978 1 84953 425 3
£9.99
Hardback

The most affectionate creature
in the world is a wet dog.
Ambrose Bierce

Dogs can be boisterous, obedient, loyal and downright lazy! This book, which brings together stories, tips, trivia, quotations and poetry celebrating all the fascinating features of the dog, is for anyone whose tail starts wagging at the thought of relaxing with a good read and a warm, cuddly canine at their feet.

DOGS

A PORTRAIT IN PICTURES AND WORDS

CHARLOTTE FRASER

DOGS
A Portrait in Pictures and Words

Charlotte Fraser

ISBN: 978 1 84953 454 3
£12.99
Hardback

To sit with a dog on a hillside on a glorious afternoon is to be back in Eden...

MILAN KUNDERA

A dog is a creature of love. Their never-ending loyalty and boundless enthusiasm is the light in any dog lover's life.

This handsome photographic collection of the most eye-catching and enchanting dogs, complemented with heart-warming quotes, poems and prose, is guaranteed to captivate and charm anyone who has ever known the companionship of a dog.

I'd like to read about your very own super dogs, and hear of any tales of super dogs that you've heard about or met. Please do feel free to share them with me at **awesomesuperdogs@gmail.com**.

If you're interested in finding out more about our books, find us on Facebook at **Summersdale Publishers** and follow us on Twitter at **@Summersdale**.

www.summersdale.com